MARCO ⊕ POLO

SHANGHAI

RUSSIA

MONGOLIA

Beijing

NORTH
KOREA

SOUTH
KOREA

Tokyo

Shanghai

JAPAN

CHINA

PACIFIC
OCEAN

VIET-
NAM

Hong Kong

TAIWAN

LAOS

PHILIPPINES

The best Insider Tips → p. 4

INSIDER TIP

Best of ... → p. 6

Sightseeing → p. 26

Food & Drink → p. 56

SYMBOLS

INSIDER TIP	Insider Tip
★	Highlight
● ● ● ●	Best of ...
☼	Scenic view

☺ Responsible travel: fair
trade principles and the
environment respected

(*) Telephone numbers that
are not toll-free

PRICE CATEGORIES HOTELS

Expensive	over 1,240 Yuan
Moderate	620–1,240 Yuan
Budget	under 620 Yuan

The prices are for two people
sharing per night, excluding
breakfast

PRICE CATEGORIES RESTAURANTS

Expensive	over 160 Yuan
Moderate	80–160 Yuan
Budget	under 80 Yuan

Prices are for a typical meal,
not including drinks

On the cover: Pudong: science fiction in steel and glass p. 48 | Artists' quarter in Moganshan Lu p. 69

CONTENTS

SHOPPING → p. 66

Entertainment → p. 74

Where to stay → p. 82

Street atlas → p. 128

DID YOU KNOW?
Table tennis & pit stop
→ p. 36
Relax & Enjoy → p. 40
Books & Films → p. 51
Keep fit! → p. 54
Gourmet restaurants → p. 60
Local specialities → p. 62
Luxury hotels → p. 86
Budgeting → p. 115
Currency converter → p. 117
Weather → p. 118

MAPS IN THE GUIDEBOOK
(130 A1) Page numbers and
coordinates refer to the street
atlas
(0) Address located off the
map. Coordinates are also
given for places that are not
marked on the street atlas
Map of the surrounding area
on p. 140/141, City maps of
Hangzhou and Suzhou on
p. 142 and p. 143
A Metro map can be found inside the back cover

INSIDE BACK COVER:
PULL-OUT MAP →

PULL-OUT MAP 🛇
(🛇 A–B 2–3) Refers to the
removable pull-out map

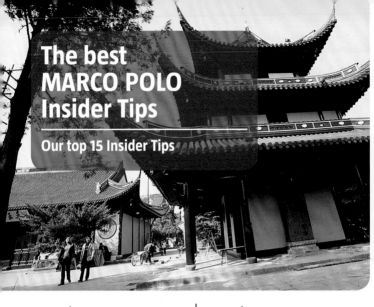

The best MARCO POLO Insider Tips

Our top 15 Insider Tips

INSIDER TIP ▶ When the red lanterns shine

Early evening in Fangbang Lu (Old China Street) is when Shanghai's contrasts are to be seen in the most beautiful light: in the foreground there are lanterns and small shops, in the distance the glittering skyscrapers → p. 34

INSIDER TIP ▶ Stylish shop

Club M1NT is the right place to see and be seen: wear something really special and classy when you dash off to enjoy the nightlife and mix with the poshest circles in the city! → p. 79

INSIDER TIP ▶ Seen literally

In the Lu Xun Museum there's a visualisation of a prose poem by the great writer — the words are beguiling, the sound of the Chinese language is utterly enchanting → p. 52

INSIDER TIP ▶ Trendsetter

In the Urbn Hotel, the old bricks of yesteryear tell the story of the design of today and the ecology of tomorrow → p. 87

INSIDER TIP ▶ A hint of Zen ...

... is what makes the masterfully executed design in the Zen Lifestore so special – and the beautiful and functional items something to embellish every home → p. 73

INSIDER TIP ▶ As beautiful as a poem

This is the experience you can relish at Hangzhou's West Lake, but only if you take a hand-steered gondola trip — incomparably superior to the hustle and bustle on the overcrowded tourist cruises → p. 94

INSIDER TIP ▶ A simple meal in a sublime place

Enjoy a delicious noodle soup in the Longhua Temple and then go and ring the bell in the adjacent tower to free yourself of all your cares and woes (photo top) → p. 51

INSIDER TIP ▶ Fashion made in Shanghai

The INSH label is symbolic of original and imaginative fashion from Shanghai — you'll find it in the International Artist Factory in the old area around Taikang Lu → p. 70

INSIDER TIP Bags for trendsetters

Wet look leather bags with gold fastener and bobbles may no doubt have a charm of their own. But Yamado's handmade purses, handbags and rucksacks tell stories of life on the steppes and in the forests → p. 71

INSIDER TIP The sound of a flute rising over the garden pond

Or an operatic aria in the pavilion – you can enjoy this and lots more of the classic Chinese art of entertainment as part of the evening cultural programme in the Wangshi Yuan (photo bottom), one of the Suzhou Classical Gardens → p. 101

INSIDER TIP New jazz in old club

Theo Croker, the young star trumpeter and composer, mixes Mississippi sound and Himalayan tones. With his sextet he gets people in the swing in the venerable jazz club at the Fairmont Peace Hotel → p. 78

INSIDER TIP Skyscrapers – yesterday and today

You can enjoy a box seat with a wonderful view of the architectural past and future from the roof terrace at Starbucks → p. 43

INSIDER TIP Pioneer work

In an old textile factory Shanghai's first green garden community is blooming: Jiashan Market. Cafés and restaurants, set up with every concern for the environment, are also a great attraction with their fresh organic food → p. 59

INSIDER TIP Underground stage

Let your fancy take flight and transport you into the fantastic world of the musical. The Shanghai Culture Square is the city's most modern concert hall → p. 81

INSIDER TIP Culture centre

The Rockbund Art Museum is a cultural centrepiece in the revitalised district by the northern Bund: enjoy looking at art and get involved → p. 32

BEST OF ...

FOR FREE

● *The amazing Shanghai Museum*

Four floors full of wonderful works of Chinese classical art and everything to be enjoyed free of charge! And you don't need to pay for the audio guide because everything's labelled in English (photo) → p. 46

● *Visit the Martyrs' Park*

If you want to understand the beginnings of communism, this is an extremely informative place to come. The extensive park is dedicated to the victims of the workers' uprising of 1927. The *Memorial Museum* documents the lives and struggles of the Red Revolutionaries → p. 52

● *Enjoyment of art in M 50 – Moganshan Lu*

It doesn't cost anything to look and you can enjoy a whole morning of perfect entertainment in this collection of galleries. There are lots of interesting works to look at. And there's always someone there with the time to chat about contemporary art in China → p. 69

● *Study life in Lu Xun Park*

A very special place where people meet to sing and dance; flute and violin music is everywhere to be heard; and the elderly practise t'ai chi ch'uan or play cards. This is where you begin to understand that the joys of living are something you can't buy, they're something you share with one another → p. 52

● *Gu Shan Island in Hangzhou*

You can enjoy the West Lake for free from the shore, but *Gu Shan* Island offers more free pleasures, with the Provincial Museum, the classical estate of the Society of Seal Arts, Sun-Yat-sen Park and the pavilion on the shore with the view known as 'Autumn Moon over the Calm Lake' → p. 95

● *Suzhou Museum*

There's no admission charge at this wonderful museum, designed for the city of his forefathers by leading architect Ieoh Ming Pei. And as a free extra you can also enjoy a modern variation on classical horticulture from the peace and quiet of a glass pavilion → p. 100

●●●● Dots in guidebook refer to 'Best of ...' tips

● *Cappuccino with a view*

The high-rise buildings in Shanghai soar into the sky. Enjoying a cappuccino in the *100 Century Avenue* restaurant in the Shanghai World Financial Center with the enormous metropolis and the broad Huangpu River at your feet, looking down on the wonderful Jin Mao Building, is a fantastic and unique experience → p. 60

● *Gourmet food à la Shanghai*

Wow! The food at *Yè Shanghai* is sooo good! You should delight your taste buds at least once with delicacies which are so typical of this city. The people here simply know what tastes good, so take their advice! → p. 64

● *Stroll through the Chinese Old City*

Get away from the beaten tourist track and head into the narrow alleys of the Old City, following their tantalising twists and turns. Say hello to the old women, wrapped up nice and warm, sitting in canvas chairs knitting, and enjoy a chat at the Old Gentlemen's Club. Wherever you go you'll encounter the friendliness so typical of Shanghai! (photo) → p. 33

● *Bar with Pudong panorama*

It's true the cocktails on the Bund are expensive, but nowhere near as outrageous as the prices in New York, Tokyo or London. In the *New Heights* bar you also get a fantastic panoramic view of the sparkling Pudong skyline → p. 79

● *Hangzhou: stroll along the Su Causeway*

It's the causeways which make the *West Lake* so special that even Beijing's emperors sought to emulate it. You can walk across the lake on them and keep your feet dry. The Su Causeway is the longer of the two, but in this case it's a question of more effort equals more enjoyment → p. 95

● *Suzhou: lose your way in Liu Yuan*

The most convoluted of the classical gardens, it offers the most surprises with its many inner courtyards, large and small, and is typical of the refinement of *Suzhou garden architecture*. You can't really get lost, but getting a little confused adds a certain frisson to the whole pleasure → p. 98

ONLY IN

BEST OF ...

AND IF IT RAINS
Activities to brighten your day

● **Warming Shanghai cuisine**
If it's dark, dank and depressing outside, then the best place is the *Xiang Zhang Garden* restaurant with steaming bowls in front of you and a view out onto Hengshan Lu → p. 64

● **Banana leaf music in the Yu Yuan**
Listen to the sound of the raindrops on the large banana leaves. That's why these perennials were planted here within hearing distance of colonnades and pavilions so that you can keep dry whilst enjoying being outside → p. 36

● **Racing cars in the rain**
A pit stop is what's needed when the first drops start to fall on the *Shanghai International Circuit* in Anting. There's a rapid tyre change and it makes the Formula I race course all the more exciting for the spectators → p. 36

● **Enjoy some retail therapy**
Whatever the weather, souvenir hunters will be in heaven here. But on rainy days it's almost cosy in the *Yuyuan Bazaar*, when it's nowhere near as crowded as usual → p. 73

● **Tea museum in Hangzhou**
A rain shower is the perfect complement to the *Tea Museum* because the plantations you look out onto love the heavenly rainfall which makes the leaves glisten. If you've finished your visit and it's still raining, then go and enjoy a tea tasting (photo) → p. 93

● **Canglang Ting Garden in Suzhou**
One thing's for certain: when it rains, each of the classical gardens reveals its own particular charm. But it's only in the *Canglang Ting* that the colonnades lead not only from building to building but take you all the way round the garden. So you can walk outside without getting wet → p. 98

RAIN

RELAX AND CHILL OUT
Take it easy and spoil yourself

● *Enjoy a relaxing massage*
If you've ever had a massage at the hands of an experienced master, you won't want to miss out ever again and, wherever you are, you'll long for a Chinese massage parlour. Try out the *Congen Massage Healthcare Club* which is very popular with the locals → **p. 40**

● *Enjoy a cocktail on the beach*
Yes, you really can! At the *Sunny Beach* in the Cool Docks you can savour your sundowner in a deck chair beneath a parasol and watch the river boats lazily drifting past (photo) → **p. 75**

● *Chill out in the jacuzzi*
The *Vue Bar* is famous not only because of its view of the Bund and Pudong. In good weather there are comfortable recliners on the terrace inviting you to relax and dangle your feet in a cooling jacuzzi → **p. 79**

● *Luxury spa*
Find peace in the Peace Hotel. That's certainly possible in one of the most luxurious spas in the city, the *Willow Stream Spa*. A massage with fragrant oils eases away all your tension in a quite wonderful way. And afterwards you can have a paddle in the pool under the glass roof and look forward to the evening rejuvenated → **p. 86**

● *Wanghu Lou Teahouse in Hangzhou*
In Hangzhou there's no more typical way to relax than over a cup of Dragon Well tea by the West Lake, for example in the 'Lake View' teahouse. And don't order the cheapest; the expensive ones are definitely much more enjoyable → **p. 96**

● *Tingfeng Yuan Garden in Suzhou*
Actually all the gardens in Suzhou would be great for relaxing if it weren't for the constant throng of visitors. But you can escape the noise in the small, less well-known estates such as this, and there's a tea counter to round off your visit. China doesn't get any nicer than this → **p. 99**

INTRODUCTION

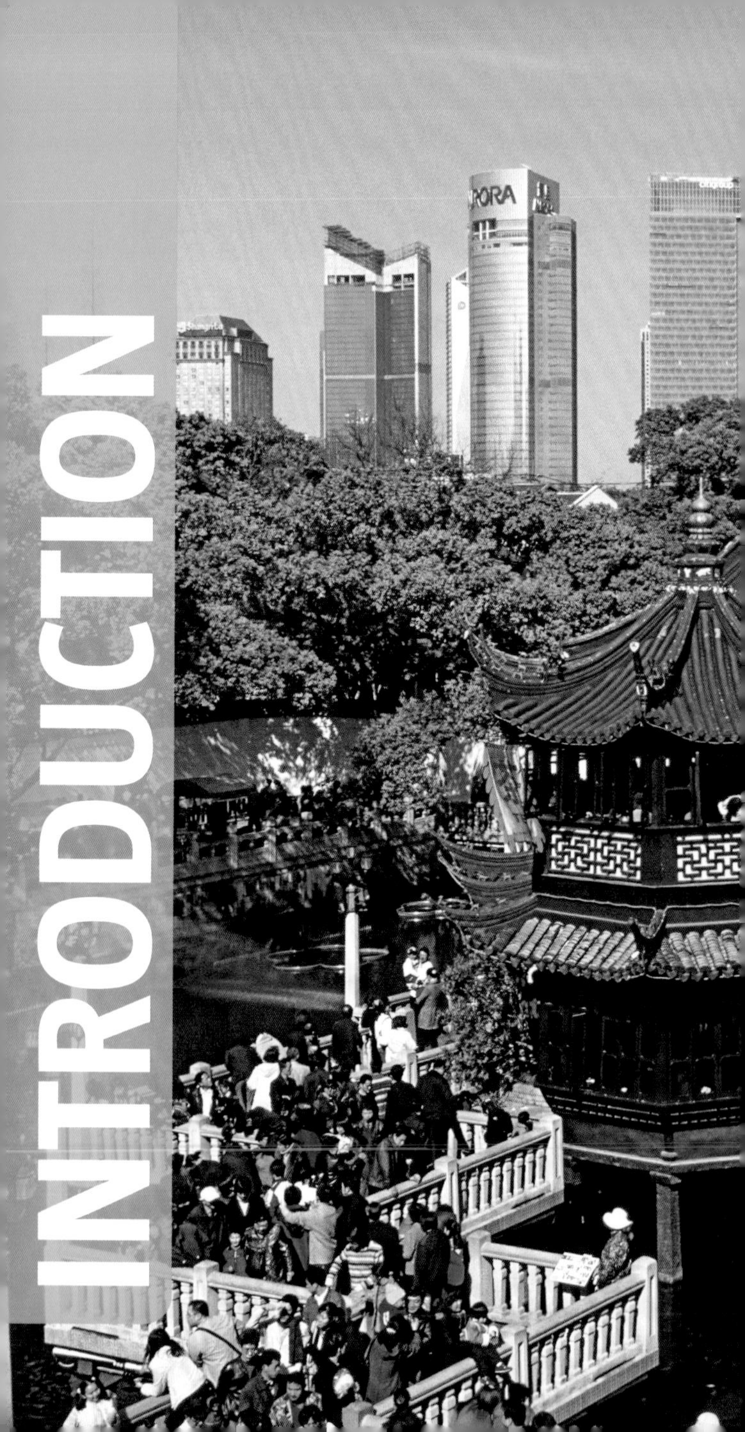

DISCOVER SHANGHAI!

As the sun rises over the city you ideally need to be standing on the River Promenade along the old Bund. There you'll be greeted by the deep horns of the Yangtze ferries and the chugging of the barges dragging behind them heavily loaded skiffs on the languidly flowing Huangpu River. You will feel welcome amongst the people practising their Qigong with rapt devotion or starting the day with a tango. You simply have to experience for yourself how the magnificent colonial buildings, relics of a great but by-gone era, emerge from the nocturnal shadows, as over there, on the far river bank a skyline slowly emerges from the morning mist, redolent of a science fiction movie. China, with 1.34 billion people the most highly populated country on the planet, is securing its place in the global economy and international politics. The huge empire is determined to be a world leader and Shanghai is playing a leading role. Intoxicated by the unrelenting redevelopment on such a massive scale, one soon runs out of superlatives. The city is proud of being home to two of the tallest skyscrapers in the

Photo: Huxinting teahouse and the Pudong skyline

world, of the very challenging Formula 1 circuit – and of the fastest train, the Transrapid, which hurtles its way to and from Pudong Airport along a maglev (magnetic levitation) track. The city reinvented itself for the World Expo 2010, razing to the ground a dilapidated industrial and residential district on both sides of the river in order to build exhibition halls, and Shanghai was transformed into an ultramodern city that lived up to the motto of 'Better City, Better Life'.

It's only when you mingle with the people that you really become aware for the first time that you're in China. The Shanghai conurbation has about 23 million inhabitants – an urban population in constant movement: the endless stream of pedestrians in Nanjing Lu, the masses of commuters in the crowded buses, and the swarms of cyclists. The people of Shanghai work tirelessly, shop incessantly and eat constantly and everywhere, or so it seems. It's only in the alleys of the Old City that life unfolds at a more modest pace. When the sun's shining, washing is dried on long poles, with underwear dangling from wires strung between the trees lining the street. The local residents put tables and chairs in the alleys and spread out their duvets on them to air. Old women knit, hawkers sleep in their favourite chairs, men crouch over board games.

> **The people of Shanghai –
> an urban population constantly
> on the move**

If you then look back to the skyline, you'll see the Jin Mao Building sparkling in the sun, this elegant tower of glass and steel, as graceful as a pagoda. With its 421m (1,381ft) it is one of the tallest buildings in the world and arguably one of the most

A wide range of offers: Nanjing Lu is the megacity's main shopping street

beautiful. It puts all the other adjacent skyscrapers in the shade, even its immediate neighbour, the Shanghai World Financial

Center, which is 71m (233ft) higher and is actually a really elegant building in its own right. Next to these two Pudong landmarks, work on a unique new structure to complete a trio of buildings is progressing: the Shanghai Tower is to reach its intended height of 632m (2,073ft) by 2014 and become the second tallest building in the world. It's the first completely 'green' high-rise building in the world, having been planned with full regard to ecological considerations and is thus a cause for hope. One wonders whether the dynamic Chinese spirit, which the building seeks to symbolise with its twisted shape, will in future show greater consideration for nature. That has not been the case over the last ten years, with more than 3,000 high-rise buildings with a height greater than 35m (115ft) having been erected on Shanghai's unstable subsoil.

There's been a similarly breath-taking dynamism once before in the history of Shanghai when, in the 19th century, the British were quick to appreciate the outstanding economic and geographical location of the city as both port and manufacturing centre. To the north of the city the Huangpu River flows into the Yangtze. This mighty river was the way to unlock the interior of this huge country and grant access to its important goods: tea, porcelain and silk. The British fought the Opium War in 1842 to open up the harbour for international trade. Together with the Americans and the French, they established their trading houses on the Huangpu and thus initiated the rapid development that saw Shanghai become one of the biggest cities in the world.

The ‹golden age› from 1900 to 1941 saw the erection of the colonial buildings on the Bund, the department stores on Nanjing Lu, the elegant clubhouses, Art Deco hotels and the residences in the French Concession. You can gain a sense of the grandeur of that period by taking a stroll along the old boulevards lined with plane trees, peeping over garden walls or peering through wrought iron fences: in gardens left to grow wild you'll see villas with oriel windows, towers and columned entrances, with folding doors leading out onto shady verandas. Photographs from that time show that the rich knew how to celebrate on special occasions.

Shanghai was honoured with the title 'Paris of the East' on account of its elegance, but was also known as the 'Whore of the Orient' because of the dubious reputation it acquired for being the wickedest city in the Far East. An army of labourers grafted away here under appalling conditions in order to create its economic success. Every morning the bodies of beggars who had starved to death were collected. Resentment about the conditions steadily increased amongst the students and educated and the Communist Party of China was founded in the French Concession in 1921. In the 'Shanghai Massacre' of April 1927, Chiang Kai-shek put down the workers' movement and the Communists fled to the mountains. This was followed by a further ten years of unbridled economic growth. Around 60,000 foreigners from more than 30 countries were living here when, after months of bombardment, the Japanese occupied the city with its 3.7 millions inhabitants in 1937. This marked the beginning of Shanghai's decline.

After years of civil war, the Communists marched into in Shanghai in 1949. Gambling was forbidden, brothels were closed down, drug addicts and prostitutes were 're-educated', slums cleared and child labour became a thing of the past. No one went hungry any more, other than with a hunger for freedom – with the government in Beijing pulling all the strings. As far as Shanghai was concerned, it was a matter of ridding the city of capitalist ideology, bourgeois behaviour and western decadence. Used to subordination from the colonial period, the people of Shanghai now marched into the factories to the sound of the sirens and produced the best products in the whole country without raking in any of the profits. Shanghai served Beijing as a 'cash cow'. At some point the once proud city was gone. The soot from all the factories had blackened the houses with grime, and indoctrination had taken away the voice of the people in their grey concrete prefabs.

The belief in progress is demonstrated in concrete, steel and glass

With the liberalisation in the 1980s the socialist dreariness began to disappear from Shanghai too, but it wasn't until 1992 that the city was able to develop freely. Billions were invested in the infrastructure, with a Special Economic Zone in Pudong attracting foreign investors. Whole districts had to give way to high-rise office blocks. Noisy and smelly factories were relocated, making way for residential areas and parks. On People's Square the Opera House was erected, heralding the return of glamour and entertainment. The futuristic TV Tower, Oriental Pearl Tower, became the highly visible symbol of the new city. Entrepreneurial energy, suppressed for so many years, has now asserted itself once more, and belief in progress is manifested in concrete, steel and glass.

In the resurrected metropolis there's no longer any room for picturesque Old City districts. Amnesty International estimates that 2.5 million residents were relocated to satellite towns in the course of the urban redevelopment from 1990 to 2003 alone. Many today enjoy better living conditions because they have moved out of unlit and cramped hovels into apartments with bathroom and kitchen and which provide each occupant with a living area of 10m². But this has been paid for by the break up of established neighbourhoods, and the sense of community has been lost. But there's no place for sentiment in Shanghai either. What counts in post-communist China is money. If you're clever, you can make a fortune here. The gold rush atmosphere is luring Chinese people from America and Hong Kong back to the land of their fathers. The young Chinese from abroad speak perfect English and dress more extravagantly than their fellow Chinese, which is how you can recognise them in the elite Club *M1NT*. The nouveaux riches make an ostentatious display of their wealth: the Mercedes S-class sells like hot cakes in Shanghai.

Shanghai shows its leisurely side with a game of cards in People's Park

Whilst the rich dine in exclusive restaurants, the workers graft away on the building sites under the harsh light of the floodlights. Itinerant workers, of whom there are approximately 5 million living in the city, do this tough, dangerous work. 'The Economist' has referred to them as slaves because they have no rights and are ruthlessly exploited. But when they have work they're better off than in the rural provinces they fled from. That China is still a developing country is easy to forget in Shanghai. Many of its citizens have never had it so good. They work hard and believe in the future again. The fear of the arbitrariness of state control is disappearing and new freedoms of thought, speech and action are growing.

> The most exciting metropolis in the world

Irrepressible creative drive, original and imaginative art and a vibrant culture, everything that's new in China is being tried out here, which is what makes Shanghai the most exciting city in the world. It is the people whose inexhaustible energy is making the metropolis pulsate to the beat of the future. In the evenings on the Bund you can sense their cheerful optimism, in the evenings when night falls in Shanghai, wonderful and sparkling and electric, making the city something truly beautiful.

WHAT'S HOT

1 Art District

New art in old halls Former warehouses have been transformed into hotspots for art, a good example being the *North Bund Art Zone (Yangshupu Lu 2361)* which houses the *Yibo Gallery (www.yibo-art.com)* and the *Fu Xin Gallery (www.fuxingallery.com.cn, photo)*. In *Warehouse No. 713 (Dong Daming Lu 713)* with galleries such as the *Ddm Warehouse (www.ddmwarehouse.org)*, *Dong Daming Art Centre* and *Endless International Art Center* you can come across newcomers through constantly changing exhibitions.

2 Bohemian Shanghai

Shanghai does Style They call themselves the 'Bohemian Generation' and do their shopping in boutiques in the north of the Xuhui district. Shanghai's fashion elite cultivates its street style in designer consortiums such as the *Creative Bazaar (bazaar.creative.googlepages.com)*. If you fancy emulating their style, then get yourself to *Eno,* the shop for 'home-grown street wear', a vibrant shopping oasis *(Changle Lu 139-23, www.eno.cn, photo)*. You'll find the matching accessories at *Christine Tsui Fashion Club (Xinle Lu 24)*.

3 Desserts to the power of three

Sweet Shanghai Light and less sweet Chinese desserts are experiencing a boom. If you dare, you should try the Tofu pudding from *Sweet Dynasty (Huaihai Zhonglu 300)*. Not quite so unusual are the creations of *Ichido (e.g. Super Brand Mall, Lujiazui Xilu 168, www.ichido.com.cn)*. You can also enjoy delicious oriental desserts such as sweet soups or dim sum at *Honeymoon Dessert (e.g. Joy City Shopping Mall, Xizang Beilu 166, www.honeymoon-dessert.com)* and at *Bellagio (Shuicheng Lu, www.bellagio cafe.com.cn)*.

Bicycle boom

Novel ideas Shanghai wants to become more bike-friendly and soon be able to call itself 'Bike City'. One initiative seeking to make a contribution is the recently introduced *bike sharing system*. You can hire a bike at a number of stations *(www.chinarmb.com)* on payment of a small deposit and with minimal charges. If you want to be even more environmentally friendly, you can hire a bike made of bamboo. *Shanghai bamboo bikes* are made completely in accordance with the customer's specifications *(www.shanghaibamboobike.com)*. Susan Evan is also concerned about sustainability and a green future, which is why she has founded the organisation *Kplunk* which, with initiatives like *Coolbike Ride*, is attempting to make cycling more popular *(www.kplunk.com, photo)*.

4

Camping in the city

Experience nature Skyscrapers, traffic, crowded streets and densely packed housing – more and more people in Shanghai want to escape life in a big city and experience the great outdoors. So a camping trip is just the job. Yes, that's right: even around one of the biggest cities in the world there are campsites. Far away from the noise of the city in *Dongping National Forest Park* you can camp in an idyllic location by Huangpu River *(Chongming Island, follow the signs)*. Closer to the city but still in the country, *Meadowbrook Equestrian and Rural Activity Center* offers adventure, nature and a campsite for you to spend the night *(Shenzhuan Gonglu 2780, Qingpu, www.meadowbrookshanghai.com, Foto)*. You can get the proper equipment such as tent, pegs and sleeping bag at *Yehuo Outdoor Outfitter (Changle Lu 296, Luwan District, www.yehuo.com)*.

5

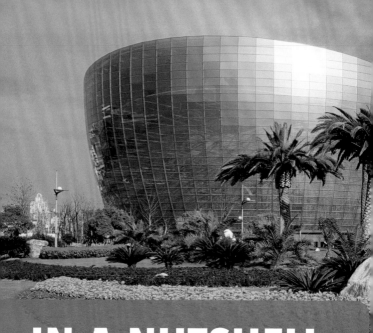

IN A NUTSHELL

BUILDINGS FOR BRIDES

In Pudong the high-rise buildings seem to be reaching for the stars, and beyond the office block towers there is the ever expanding sprawl of the concrete jungle: the apartment blocks stand in file, street after street and as high as the sky. There is so much available and yet people are groaning under rising property prices. Whilst the ratio of income to expenditure on food has improved, living costs are tearing an ever greater hole in the family budget.

And the fathers of Shanghai comment with a snarl that it's the new generation of daughters who are to blame. Instead of moving in meek and mild with their husband's parents as their mothers once did, and being under the mother-in-law's thumb, they're demanding an apartment of their own as a wedding present! And because Shanghai women are not only lovely but also assertive, their suitors lay this concrete wedding gift at their feet.

DRAGONS

Dragons are not monsters to be feared in China but well-loved symbols of good fortune. Shanghai enjoys the popular nickname of the 'dragon's head on the Yangtze': annual economic growth has for years been one of the highest in the world, standing at more than ten percent. Around 10,000 foreign firms maintain a base in the Pudong banking and business district, including companies such as Astra-Zeneca, Dow Chemical,

Photo: Shanghai Oriental Art Center

Pyjamas and designer clothes: fashions and other remarkable features from the new Asian capital

Ford, General Electric, IBM, Price Waterhouse and Westinghouse.

FOREIGNERS

After the First Opium War of 1839–42 the British, Americans and French obtained exterritorial rights for their commercial settlements. The foreigners formed a state within a state with its own government, jurisdiction, fiscal sovereignty and protection forces. Whilst the French had their Concession administered by a General Consul, the British

and Americans merged theirs to create the 'International Settlement'. The city with the most modern infrastructure in the Orient drew people from all levels of society and all countries. The safety of the concessions also made them a refuge for Chinese fleeing from rebellion and arbitrary rule.

In 1930 there were about 1 million Chinese and 50,000 foreigners living in the concessions, the majority of the foreigners being the Japanese, followed by the British and lots of Russians, who'd emigrated after the 1917 October Revolution, and also Americans and French. In 1937 the Japanese occupied the Hongkou district and in 1941 they also occupied the International Settlement and interned the members of the allied powers. In 1943 the western powers renounced their rights. After the seizure of power by the Communist Party in 1949 the foreigners had to leave the city.

Today there are 200,000 foreigners living in the Shanghai conurbation and Yangtze Delta, the three largest contingents being Japanese, American and Korean, which together account for more than half of the total.

GREEN GANG

This underground organisation controlled the vice dens of Shanghai in the 1920s and 1930s. The handsome profits from gambling, pimping and the drugs trade ended up in the pockets of its leader, Du Yuesheng. The Chinese godfather allegedly ruled over 20,000 Mafiosi and was also involved in politics. In 1927, the Green Gang was complicit in the brutal murders of communists and rebellious workers. Members of the gang infiltrated the international and French police. Du Yuesheng acquired Portuguese nationality in order to escape the clutches of the Chinese authorities.

Breathtaking economic growth: ultramodern architecture in Pudong

The gangster assumed a facade of respectability by investing in legal businesses and dining with the heads of industry and top bankers. A gala dinner in 1933 ended with all the guests complaining of a stomach upset and three of the invited guests of honour, including the French Consul General, later died of poisoning. In his old age the infamous Du devoted himself to Christian charity work and he died a millionaire in Hong Kong in 1951.

JEWISH REFUGEES

During the Nazi period some 20,000 German and European Jews fled to Shanghai. The city was the only place in the world which took in Jewish refugees without a passport and visa. The first arrivals were still able to build a new life in 1930s, but all the 'stateless people' who arrived after 1938 were interned by the Japanese in 1943 and confined in a ghetto to the north of Huangpu. Not allowed to work, many starved to death during the last years of the war and after the Japanese capitulation in 1945 the survivors left the country, many going to the United States, including Michael Blumenthal, later to become the US Secretary of the Treasury and now the director of the Jewish Museum in Berlin. An exhibition in the Ohel Moishe Synagogue erected by the Russians in 1907 provides a reminder of these times.

OPIUM

At the end of the 18th century the English hit on the idea of illegally importing cheap opium from India into China and using the profits to finance their tea imports. The heavy demand for opium bled the rich and industrially highly developed China dry, and drug addiction had a demoralising effect on society. When an imperial official in Canton had British opium destroyed, England seized upon this as a justification for war (First Opium War 1839–42). In defeat, China was forced to open up Hong Kong, Shanghai and other ports to free trade as well as granting privileges to the foreigners in their commercial settlements. Many of Shanghai's 'first families' founded their wealth on opium smuggling. The communists brought a temporary end to the trade in 1949. Today's underground, the Chinese triads, now deal in refined opium: heroin.

PYJAMAS

'Uncivilised!' was what the government in Beijing thought of the Shanghai custom of setting off for an evening stroll round the shops in pyjamas. And so for the World Expo 2010 a decree was issued banning pyjamas: gentlemen in pyjamas with loud patterns and ladies in frilly nylon nighties were not to be allowed to ruin the city's cosmopolitan image. The ban met with much criticism around the world and gave rise to the foundation of the Pyjama Party which wants to prevent the demise of the charming custom.

In the late 1970s, with the opening up to the west, the people of Shanghai also adopted pyjamas. Whoever could afford such a smart item of clothing as night wear, was of course only too proud to show it off – privacy within one's own home was in any case pretty much impossible in the densely populated Old City districts. Pyjamas were considered cool, as indeed they were in the muggy summer months. The casual pyjama life of that time is documented by Justin Guariglia in his volume of photos *Planet Shanghai.* Nowadays you would be hard pushed to find anyone wearing their pyjamas outside, except perhaps for some dogged old gentleman in his backyard. But rumour has it that recently, right in the middle of Nanjing Lu, two young rebels were seen in silk pyjamas.

RELIGION

In the new Shanghai, materialistic and with a focus on the here and now, you would not at first expect to detect much in the way of devoutness. But modern life is richly endowed with imponderables, whether dangers on the roads or risks on the stock exchange. And that's why, after the end of the Mao era, even the major cities were happy once more to turn heavenwards for support. However, it has to be said that the people of Shanghai are quite restrained in how they deal with these matters, and rarely will you encounter ostentatious demonstrations of devoutness. The attitude you'll most often come across with regard to making sacrifices or praying is that 'You can't be too careful' and 'It can't do any harm'. The Jade Buddha Temple in particular earns a great deal of money through donations and performing funeral ceremonies. The state gives no regular financial support for the running and maintenance of the monasteries even though the monks are employed by the state. There has also been a strong tradition of the practice of Christianity in Shanghai. The most popular religion is, of course, Buddhism but, since there is no established Buddhist church, there are no reliable statistics.

SASSOON

In the Shanghai of old you could make a fortune or finish up in the gutter. Among the most successful soldiers of fortune were the Sassoons, starting with Elias Sassoon who came to the city in 1844 from India, where his father, a Jewish merchant from Baghdad, had already made a fortune. Elias made his fortune by trading cotton and opium. Even more famous was his grandson Ellice Victor (1881–1961) who made huge profits as a banker, property magnate and bon viveur. The Peace Hotel building once bore his name when it was known as Sassoon House. After a flying accident whilst serving with the Royal Flying Corps during the First World War, he walked on crutches. He did not marry until quite old since he assumed, probably with some justification, that women were more interested in his money than in him.

SHANGHAI GIRLS

Shanghai's women are chic: the older ones because they enjoy the freedom of wearing pumps instead of fabric shoes; and the younger ones because they can easily slip into fake designer clothes by Gucci, Prada and Chanel thanks to their extensive availability. Wearing dramatic skimpy dresses is important

ment – and 280 industrial plants were cleared. These measures were taken to reinforce Shanghai's status as a world city and financial centre and to attract investors, to whom Shanghai offers not only an outstanding infrastructure but

China's Expo Pavilion: in Pudong a new residential and business district is to be created

for women who think marrying a rich man is a goal worth striving for. Foreigners are particularly in demand because they are basically considered to be well off, which is why it can be very hard, as a male tourist out on an evening pub crawl, to escape from the constant proposition 'Buy me a drink!'

WORLD EXPO

Shanghai prepared for Expo 2010 with an extraordinary show of financial muscle, spending a total of some 35 billion GBP/55 billion US$. The metro was extended from two to 13 lines, two new airport terminals, runways, bridges, roads and promenades were built and every visible nook and cranny of the city renovated. 18,000 families were relocated – which did not escape critical com-

also one very special attribute: which other megacity could boast of an availability of building land measuring 3.3 sq mi in a perfect location by the river? Some of the buildings erected for World Expo in Pudong, such as the Expo Axis, the Mercedes Benz Arena and the Chinese Pavilion are to provide the core for a state-of-the-art, exclusive residential and business district. And the creators of the first 'green' World Expo will be hoping that at least some of the 73 million Expo visitors – 95% of whom came from China – have taken on board and might even start to implement some of what they saw by way of ideas for sustainable living in a planned city that is both people and environment friendly. But it remains to be seen how great the impact of the 'Green Expo' has in fact been.

THE PERFECT DAY
Shanghai in 24 hours

07:00am EARLY MORNING SPORT IN FUXING PARK

The Chinese like to meet up early in the park so that they can do all the things there they can't do at home in their cramped living rooms, like practise taijiquan (elegant shadow boxing) or mulanji (gymnastics with swords) and dance the tango to music from their cassette recorders. If you've had a good night's sleep, you can start the day with them in *Fuxing Park → p. 39* (photo left).

07:45am THROUGH THE FRENCH CONCESSION

Go for a short walk through the *French Concession → p. 37*. The lively Nancang Lu is especially lovely in the early morning light. Stroll down the street to Xiangyang Lu where you keep right, cross Huaihai Lu and turn into Donghu Lu. The café restaurant *Wagas → p. 65* is a popular place where young foreign visitors to Shanghai come to meet up. Crispy bread, French croissants, delicious sandwiches and excellent coffee make it a good port of call for breakfast.

09:15am TO PEOPLE'S SQUARE

Go to the Shanxi Road South metro station, which is just a few minutes' walk away in Huaihai Lu, and take the M1 in the direction of *People's Square → p. 42*. Arriving so early in the day, you should be able to get free tickets for the *Shanghai Museum → p. 46*, that wonderful museum of classical Chinese art and culture with fabulous displays of ancient bronzes, ceramics, porcelain, jades and watercolours. Have a look in the museum shop to see if they have a copy of your favourite item. At *Starbucks → p. 43* on People's Square you can enjoy a great location with a view of the high-rise Park Hotel and Tomorrow Square buildings.

00:15pm INTO THE CHINESE OLD CITY

If you're a good walker, you can easily walk from People's Square via *Mu'en Church → p. 43* to the district behind the Bund, and from here make your way along Yunnan Zhonglu to the *Chinese Old City → p. 33*. Or you can take M8 to the Dashijie station. A short detour into the classically beautiful *Yu Yuan → p. 35* garden is well worth while, if only for its soothing effect on the senses as it lives up to its name as the 'Garden of Happiness'. At midday you can enjoy deliciously light dim sum in the gallery of the *Nanxiang Steamed Buns Restaurant → p. 63* (but make sure to book first!) and observe the lively hustle and bustle in the *Yuyuan Bazaar → p. 73* (photo right).

See Shanghai at its best – close up, without the stress yet all in one day

02:45pm STROLL ALONG NANJING LU

From the Yu Garden station now take the M10 to Nanjing Road East. Stroll along the Nanjing Lu shopping street heading towards the Bund and look in awe and amazement at the huge range of goods on offer – and the vast numbers of shoppers. The one-hour tour of the *Peace Hotel* → p. 32 is worthwhile, enabling you not only to savour an aesthetic sense of the golden 1930s, but also to immerse yourself in the history of the legendary hotel. Afternoon tea in the Jasmin Lounge is the perfect way to round off this marvellous experience.

05:45pm TUNNEL TRIP TO PUDONG

Walk along the Bund promenade heading north so that you can then hurtle through the Bund Sightseeing Tunnel to *Pudong* → p. 48 (photo top). There you can stroll along the Promenade southwards. Turn into Huayuanshiqiao Lu heading towards the skyscrapers. Whether from the observatory on the *Jin Mao Building* → p. 49 (cheaper!) or on the *Shanghai World Financial Center* → p. 50 (higher!), the view is breathtaking and in the golden evening light an unforgettable experience.

08:00pm DINNER ON THE BUND

Then jump in a taxi and let yourself be chauffeured back to the Bund before treating yourself to dinner at *Mr & Mrs Bund* → p. 60 and wine and dine in fine style with a wonderful view of the glittering Pudong skyline.

10:00pm NOW FOR THE NIGHTLIFE

Jazz or rock? That's now the question. It's only a stone's throw to the *House of Blues and Jazz* → p. 78, so make sure you drop in and have a listen. If it's rock you fancy, you need to head for the *Yu Yin Tang* → p. 80. The best way to get there is on the M2 from Nanjing West Road to Zhongshan Park where you change to the M3 or M4 to get to Yan'an Road West. The night is yet young!

Metro to the starting point: M1
Stop: Huangpi Road South
Practical: use the Shanghai Public Transportation Card to pay on the Metro and in the taxi without using cash

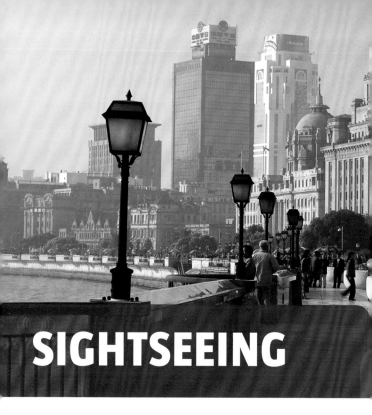

SIGHTSEEING

CITY **WHERE TO START?**
People's Square **(134 A3)**
(*M6–7*): recognisable from a distance by the pyramidal spire of Tomorrow Square (284m/932ft), Shimao Plaza (333m/1,093ft) and Park Hotel (84m/276ft). Monumental buildings such as the Opera House, Town Hall and the Shanghai Museum give a first impression of Shanghai's modernity. The square is an important metro interchange. You get to it on lines M1, M2 and M8, which will also take you from here, sometimes with a change, to all the sights. You can cross Nanjing Lu to get to the River Promenade and the Bund.

When you arrive in Shanghai, you'll be quite literally speechless: a sea of buildings as far as the eye can see.

The best place to get a first impression of the megacity is from a great height: from the TV Tower observation deck, from the Jin Mao Building or the Shanghai World Financial Center. A drive along the Yan'an Lu main street will give you a glimpse down into deep canyons of streets densely lined with buildings. You can take a boat trip to explore the glorious and newly rich city waterfront, the Bund and Pudong. A visit to a museum is also worthwhile because you simply must have a look at ancient Chinese art, the city's history and its vision for the future. The sights are, as a rule, open every day, but usually close quite early (4–5pm). The best way to experi-

Photo: view of the Bund

Shanghai is one of the most exciting places on earth: an extraordinary jewel in the conurbation on the Yangtze delta

ence the city's contrasts is on foot: you'll come across old and new, Chinese and Western, rural and urban, old-communist and capitalist, they're all to be found here, cheek by jowl. And should you get lost or your feet begin to ache, just jump into a taxi - there are 45,000 of them!

Also, there's no need to be anxious as you go out and about in the evening because Shanghai is a pretty safe city, though you should be on your guard against pickpockets in the pedestrian areas and shopping centres. But beware: it only takes an hour

or two and you'll feel almost intoxicated by the sights and sounds of this city which bustles with energy and vitality. Considered in the cold light of day and compared with Beijing, what some people say may well be true: that there aren't any major tourist attractions in Shanghai. But it isn't China's imperial past that makes the city worth seeing, rather the future being inexorably built here day and night. Shanghai's greatest attraction is Shanghai itself. When there's a metro station within walking distance of an address, it's mentioned below.

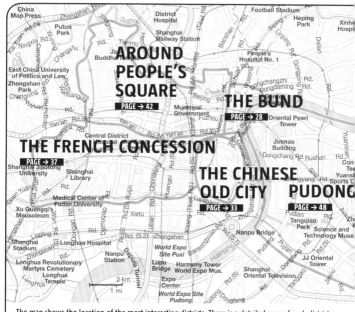

The map shows the location of the most interesting districts. There is a detailed map of each district on which each of the sights described is numbered.

THE BUND

外滩

★ 🔅 **The Anglo-Indian expression for a man-made river embankment has become a synonym for the most impressive riverside promenade in the Far East.** Shanghai's glorious past and its burgeoning future face each other across the banks of the broad Huangpu River. Over in Pudong the symbolic Oriental Pearl TV Tower rises up like a Martian spaceship and the Shanghai World Financial Center, the Jin Mao Building and the soon to be completed Shanghai Tower dominate the modern skyline. On this side of the river the stone relics from the colonial past are evidence of the power and wealth of the

banks and great trading houses which once resided here. Punished by the communists with neglect, these mighty monuments hewn from granite are now once again some of the most expensive properties in the city. Their window displays are a eulogistic celebration of fabulous prosperity. Posh restaurants and sophisticated bars, exclusive shops and fine galleries are there to satisfy every need of the rich. The River Promenade was raised in 1992 to protect against floods, which led to the felling of the beautiful trees that can be seen on old photos in the *Bund Historical Museum (Beneath the Monument to the People's Heroes | daily 9am–4.30pm | admission free)*. The Huangpu Park has been extended to accommodate exhibitions by diverting traffic on the Zhongshan Dong

Yilu through a tunnel. This has been really good for the popular promenade, which now benefits from the magnificent backdrop and is brought to life by the many people who come to meet here. In the mornings it's the pensioners who come for a bit of exercise, peace and quiet and revitalisation, during the day it's the camera-toting tourists on their city tour, and in the evening fashionably dressed Shanghainese looking down proudly and serenely on the amazed visitors from the country. You can enjoy a lovely view of the Bund from the terrace of the *Vue Bar*, the *Glamour Bar* and the *Captain's Bar*.

The historic buildings of the city all bear stone information panels. The buildings described here are listed by location from south to north.

■ SHANGHAI CLUB 原上海总会
(135 D3) (ﾌﾞ 07)

Erected in 1910 in English Renaissance style, the building with the two small towers on the roof was the principal men's club for the British residents of Shanghai. The famous Long Bar, at 34m (112ft) allegedly the longest in the world, was where the elite members of the Shanghai Club, founded in 1864, came to drink, smoke and gossip. Noel Coward, as he placed his cheek on the bar, claimed that he could see the curvature of the earth. New members had to sit towards the end of the bar, far away from the window, having been advised that downing two large measures of whisky was just the right amount to forget all your cares and woes. Women were denied entry because they would only disturb the male company. And the Chinese were not allowed in either. The Waldorf Astoria Hotel has faithfully restored the men's *Long Bar* and constructed a women's *Salon de Ville* opposite it. *Zhongshan Dong Yilu* 中山东一路 2

■ THREE ON THE BUND 外滩三号
(135 D3) (O6)

The former Union Building with the portal on the corner of Guangdong Lu was

MARCO POLO HIGHLIGHTS

designed by the architects' office of Palmer & Turner in Hong Kong, a firm whose buildings came to characterise the city in the 1920s and 1930s, and which since 1990 has again left its mark on the city in the shape of modern skyscrapers. A rich Chinese man from America bought the run-down building, constructed in the Renaissance style in 1916. Luxury shops and exclusive restaurants have created a niche in the lifestyle market, and it's here that the new upper classes don't just buy exclusive clothes and enjoy exquisite food, but also cultivate their artistic tastes. The Shanghai Gallery of Arts has a display of contemporary art on the third floor. Zhongshan Dong Yilu 中山东一路 3

■3 HONG KONG AND SHANGHAI BANK 原汇丰银行大楼 (135 D3) (Ⅲ 06)

This enormous neoclassical building designed by Palmer & Turner with its characteristic dome immediately catches your eye. In its time the second largest bank in the world, HSBC made so much money financing trade that it was able to indulge in this showy headquarters in 1921. From 1949 to 1995 it housed the city administration, which ran the city and was responsible for its buildings. Its present tenant, the Pudong Development Bank, restored the impressive hall, the ceiling of which is supported by 13-m (43-ft) high columns made of Italian marble. The dome above the entrance is decorated with mosaics, depicting the bank's eight previous main buildings. *Mon–Fri 9am–5.30pm | Zhongshan Dong Yilu* 中山东一路 12

■4 CUSTOM HOUSE 海关大楼 (135 D3) (Ⅲ 06)

This 1927 building's distinctive clock tower is where 'Big Ching' strikes. In the old Custom House of 1843, the clock kept memories of the British homeland alive and has since protected the city from fire, or so superstitious Chinese people thought, because the god of fire, mistaking the ringing of the bells every 15 minutes for a fire alarm, decided not to start any more fires. The Custom House

Outstanding architecture on the Bund: the Custom House with its 90-m high clock tower

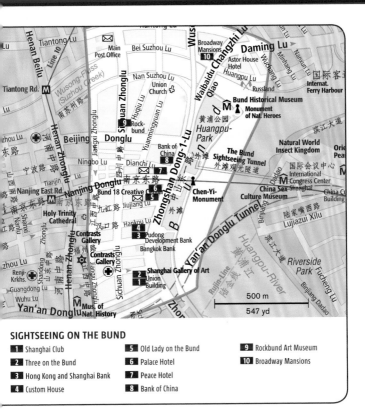

SIGHTSEEING ON THE BUND

- **1** Shanghai Club
- **2** Three on the Bund
- **3** Hong Kong and Shanghai Bank
- **4** Custom House
- **5** Old Lady on the Bund
- **6** Palace Hotel
- **7** Peace Hotel
- **8** Bank of China
- **9** Rockbund Art Museum
- **10** Broadway Mansions

also brought China tangible advantages of course: at the beginning of the 20th century, about a third of state finances were derived from income generated by maritime trade taxes. The tax authority under British management used modern methods of administration, worked efficiently and was a visible expression of the cooperation between foreign free trade and the Chinese state. *Zhongshan Dong Yilu* 中山东一路 *13*

5 OLD LADY ON THE BUND
桂林大楼 (135 D2) (*ⁿ O6*)

The slender building was the home of the oldest English-speaking newspaper

in China. The publication of the 'North China Daily News', founded in 1864, was suspended with the outbreak of the Korean War in 1951. The building, erected in 1923 in neo-Renaissance style, now has the large red letters AIA of the American International Assurance company emblazoned high on its facade. *Zhongshan Dong Yilu* 中山东一路 *17*

6 PALACE HOTEL 原汇中饭店
(135 D2) (*ⁿ O6*)

This building, erected in 1906 and one of the oldest on the Bund, is instantly recognisable with its red and white brick facade. It was where the appointment of

Sun Yat-sen as the first provisional President of the new Republic of China was celebrated in 1912. Today the Swatch Art Palace Hotel is exclusively reserved for artists who live, work and exhibit here. *Zhongshan Dong Yilu* 中山东一路 *19 | Entrance Nanjing Lu 23*

■7 PEACE HOTEL 和平饭店 ★
(135 D2) *(∅ O6)*

At the beginning of Nanjing Lu towers the former Sassoon House, crowned with a 19-m (62-ft) high copper pyramid that in the evening is resplendently illuminated in green. Designed by Palmer & Turner in 1928 in the Chicago School style, it once housed the luxurious Cathay Hotel. This is where everyone who was anyone had to stay, including stars such as Charlie Chaplin. The immeasurably rich Sir Ellice Victor Sassoon, who was responsible for its construction, occupied the penthouse. The Jewish property magnate's elegant women, his extravagant cars and the exalted parties in the nightclub under the roof are the stuff of legends. The Peace Hotel foyer is considered a masterpiece of Art Deco. The Fairmont hotel chain re-opened the magnificent building in 2010, marvellously restored to its former glory after years of work. The *Peace Gallery (daily 10am–7pm, a little hidden away, one staircase higher)* has exhibitions on the Peace Hotel's history. An English art expert provides a INSIDER TIP *Hotel Tour (approx. 110–380 Yuan | Registration on tel. 021 63 21 68 88-67 51 or peace.gallery@fairmont.com);* the tour can be combined with a light lunch at midday (Tiffin Tour) or a tea in the afternoon (High Tea Tour) in the Jasmine Lounge. *Nanjing Donglu* 南京东路 *20*

■8 BANK OF CHINA 中国银行
(135 D2) *(O6)*

Architecture in the modern style with a Western stamp was superseded in 1936 with elements of the Chinese national style, giving rise to the monumental Bank of China building (BOC). This was where the Song family held sway, acquiring enormous wealth during the rule of Chiang Kai-shek (1887–1975). The Bank of China was founded in 1912 as the republic's state bank. In 1994 it opened as a state-owned commercial bank. *Zhongshan Dong Yilu* 中山东一路 *23*

■9 INSIDER TIP ROCKBUND ART MUSEUM 上海外滩美术馆
(135 D2) *(∅ O5)*

The former Royal Asiatic Society Building, once China's first museum, now displays

LOW BUDGET

▶ You can familiarise yourself with the city by taking *bus 911* serving the route Renmin Lu **(134 B4)** *(∅ N7)*–Huaihai Lu–Hongqiao Lu. Change at Hongqiao Road Station to the Pearl Line (M3, direction Shanghai Railway Station) and go as far as the *Zhongshan Park* **(0)** *(∅ D4–5)*, which you can visit for free and which has a large collection of trees and flowers.

▶ Alternative to the expensive spas: the whole family can have a wonderful time chatting and relaxing at the *Xiaonanguo Tanghe-yuan* bathhouse. First of all the sexes are separated for bathing, massaging and rubbing with oil, then everyone comes together to eat, play or watch a piece of theatre. Admission approx. *60 Yuan, massage extra | Hongmei Lu 3337 (Near Yan'an Lu, next to Pearl City and behind the Xiaonanguo Restaurant) | M10 Longxi Road* **(0)** *(∅ O)*

Still room for some traditional hustle and bustle: shopping street in the Chinese Old City

contemporary art in the guise of the Rockbund Art Museum (RAM). It houses exhibitions, installations, live performances, film screenings and workshops, and it's here that they run an extensive and exciting programme examining modern culture – Fridays and Saturdays and sometimes even at night too. *Tue–Sun 10am–6pm | admission 10 Yuan | Huqiu Lu* 虎丘路 *20 | www.rockbundartmuseum.org | M2, M10 Nanjing Road East*

10 BROADWAY MANSIONS 上海大厦 **(135 E1)** *(*🗺️ *P5)*

The 19-storey monolith on Suzhou Creek marks the northern end of the Bund and has long been a prominent symbol of the city. The majestic terraced building constructed of dark brick was built in 1934 as an apartment house in the Chicago School style. Whilst the architecture of the older colonial buildings is very much based on European styles from Baroque to Classical to Art Nouveau and Bauhaus, the later buildings such as this or the Grosvenor House (on the plot of

the Jinjiang Hotel) reflect the American influence. Indeed, it's been said the apartment block wouldn't have looked out of place in Manhattan. *By Suzhou Lu* 北苏州路 *20*

THE CHINESE OLD CITY

老城

★ ● **On the city plan the Chinese Old City immediately grabs your attention, as it's surrounded by a circular road built to replace the city walls torn down in 1911.**

This is where the heart of the city beats – there's a lively hustle and bustle in the bazaar area, even though many of the apparently historic buildings have been rebuilt in the old style. To a great extent, you can still come across the original atmosphere in streets like *Dajing Lu* **(134 B–C 4–5)** *(*🗺️ *N8)*. Here the old two-storey houses stand closely side by side, here people live and work just as they did one hundred years ago. Informal social intercourse takes places predominantly on the doorstep – a peaceful coming together in an intimate space. In *Fangbang Lu* (Old China Street) (134–135 C–D5) *(Ꝏ O8)* you can buy souvenirs by the thousand. It's at its most beautiful here INSIDER TIP early in the evening when red lanterns illuminate the street and the small shops, and the lights in the high-rise buildings shine out in the distance. *M10 Yu Garden*

◾1 CONFUCIUS TEMPLE (WEN MIAO)
文庙 (134 B6) *(Ꝏ N9)*

In ancient China any city that was the seat of an imperial official always used to have a Confucian temple and, as a state building, it was always representative. And so it is with the Shanghai temple dating from 1855. The main hall, especially, makes a grand impression with its high curb roof. On the terrace outside,

elaborate ceremonies used to be held annually to celebrate Confucius' birthday, financed by the public purse, because Confucius (died AD 479) was highly esteemed by virtue of his office as a great teacher and founder of the concept of the state. The hall contains a statue of the master. The walls are decorated with stone tablets that contain the entire text of his Analects (Lunyu). On one side there is the two-storey library and the former temple school; at the front on the right the 'Tower of the Star of Literature' rises up over the garden pond. *Daily 9am–4.30pm | admission 10 Yuan | Wenmiao Lu* 文庙路 *215 | M8 Laoximen*

◾2 CITY GOD TEMPLE (CHENGHUANG MIAO)
城隍庙 (135 D5) *(Ꝏ O8)*

This popular temple to various patrons used to form, with the square outside, the actual centre of old Shanghai. Trashed in the Cultural Revolution and used

Rockery, water and pavilion: scenery in the classic Chinese Yu Yuan Garden

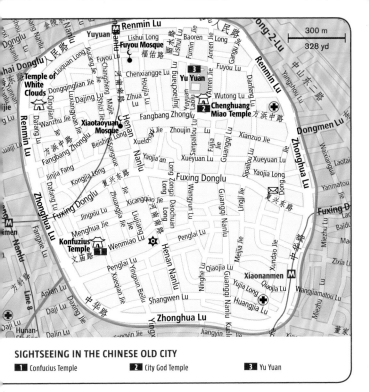

SIGHTSEEING IN THE CHINESE OLD CITY

1 Confucius Temple   **2** City God Temple   **3** Yu Yuan

as a shop, the City God Temple was re-established as a temple in the 1990s and completely restored through private donations in 2006. In the first hall you see the deified state chancellor Huo Guang (1st century AD) next to adjutants and bailiffs, in the connecting hall behind come the gods of the year belonging to the Chinese 60-year cycle. This is a place where everyone can make a sacrifice to the god of the year of his birth and thus be able to count on his support. In the following courtyard to the right stand female protective deities (offering protection, for example, for children's eyesight and seafarers), whilst in the side hall to the left Guan Di, the God of Wealth, is

honoured as a powerful patron of many trades, and also Wenchang as the protective deity of literature. The image of the red-faced city god can be seen in the last hall, to the sides his wife and parents. A shop in the temple sells lovely calligraphies. *Daily 8.30am–4.30pm | admission 10 Yuan | in the north-east of the Old City*

3 **YU YUAN** 豫园 ★ (135 D4–5) (*Ø O8*)
This is Shanghai's most important classical Chinese sight. A high-ranking official began to design the 'Garden of Happiness' from 1559 as a retreat. The current buildings were not however built until the 18th and 19th centuries when the garden, which had become overgrown, was

acquired by businessmen, and merchant guilds established their meeting rooms and living quarters here. They loved it for its folksy character: all the figures depicted that you see (including the famous dragon wall) are typical of the merchants' tastes at that time and not really suitable as a classical garden. Nonetheless, its compositional elements are realised in a virtuoso way. Take note of the juxtaposition of rocks and water, the interplay of irregularity and symmetry, the richness in form of the windows and the separation into smaller parts achieved by colonnades, walls, halls and pavilions which creates an abundance of diverse scenic landscapes over a small area.

The experience of the garden begins right at the gate, with the path over the Nine *Zigzag Bridge* past *the Huxinting Tea House*. The entrance takes you into the western part of the garden with *the Three Ears of Corn Hall*, formerly an assembly room. Behind the following hall you're now standing in front of the garden's most famous scenic landscapes. Here, beyond a pond with golden carp and water lilies, an artificial *Huge Rock-ery* made of yellow rocks rises up – the only original element from the 16th century. *The River View Pavilion* on its peak at that time justifiably bore that name. Go past the pond, then right, and you'll come to the famous Double Line Corridor. If you then go alongside the eastern garden ponds or across bridges over them towards the south, you'll see another showpiece: three rocks, the middle one of which called 'Exquisite Jade' is one of the most famous garden rocks in China, decorate the courtyard to the south in front of a hall standing on top of a high base. It's full of holes like an enormous sponge. Further to the south you come to the 'Inner Garden', which once belonged to the neighbouring City God Temple and where a beautifully decorated theatre stage has been preserved.

It can be experienced at its most beautiful when there's ● INSIDER TIP rain. First of all, the crowds are much smaller and secondly the garden is then also audible, with the characteristic 'plop' with which the raindrops fall on the leaves of banana trees, which have been planted there for that very purpose. After your visit it's time

TABLE TENNIS & PIT STOP

The main attraction for the hordes of car fanatics is the ultramodern ● *Formula 1 track (Shanghai International Circuit, Anting | www.formula1.com)* **(141 D3)** *(∅ 0)* with 200,000 seats. The Grand Prix races, first held in 2004, are also worth a visit because of the much more reasonable ticket prices in comparison with Europe. The *Shanghai Shenhua* football team plays in the Chinese Super League, roughly equivalent to the English Championship, but the matches at the *Hongkou Stadium* **(131 F1)** *(∅ P1)* are a real experience thanks to the wild *Blue Devil* fans. The stadium also has three squash courts and a climbing wall. A popular sport with a long tradition is table tennis and there's a great atmosphere when whole families give vent to their enthusiasm. And it has to be said that most of the world-class players are Chinese! *Announcements in all city magazines (See 'Travel Tips' chapter)*

to relax in the Tea House. *Daily 8.30am–5 pm (entrance until 4.30pm) | admission 40 Yuan, July/Aug and Dec–March 30 Yuan | in the north-east of the Old City*

THE FRENCH CONCESSION

法租界

The former foreign districts are attractive because they appear so intimate, and it was here, around 1900, that co-

of the Chinese town in an area measuring 6 sq mi. The quarter's main artery was *Avenue Joffre*, an elegant shopping thoroughfare with cafés and shops. The street is now Huaihai Lu, tastelessly renovated by businessmen from Taiwan and Hong Kong and sadly the Parisian ambience has been lost. The middle classes go to the department stores just to look, as it's only the nouveaux riches who can actually afford to buy anything there!

But progress has not inflicted as many wounds in the French quarter as elsewhere. Here there are countless apart-

Taking a stroll along the upscale Huaihai Lu shopping street

lonial buildings were erected to serve as a reminder of the European homelands. But it was also here that architects found a place to experiment, combining Art Deco, rational Bauhaus style or the functional modern with oriental compositional elements to create very interesting buildings. Yan'an Lu main street, as *Avenue Foch*, once used to mark the boundary between the International Settlement and the French Concession. The French lived to the south of this street and to the west

ment blocks in the Art Deco style still standing, and in shady alleys you'll find dilapidated villas emanating an antiquated colonial charm. Also worth seeing are the renovated mansions such as the hotel *Tai Yuan Villa (Taiyuan Lu 160)* (132 B5) (*⑭ H9*) and the opulent villa housing the *Shanghai Arts & Crafts Museum (Fenyang Lu 79)* (132 C4) (*⑭ H8*). Also to be found in this area are the lilongs or longtangs, the terraced courtyard houses which are so typical of

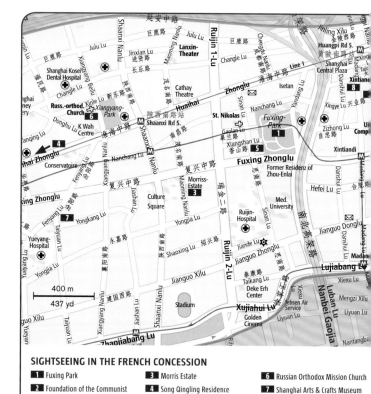

SIGHTSEEING IN THE FRENCH CONCESSION

1 Fuxing Park
2 Foundation of the Communist Party of China
3 Morris Estate
4 Song Qingling Residence
5 Sun Yat-sen Residence
6 Russian Orthodox Mission Church
7 Shanghai Arts & Crafts Museum
8 Shikumen Open House Museum

Shanghai. They were built between 1850 and 1940 principally for Chinese employees of foreign firms. Amongst the loveliest examples are the *Verdun Garden* built in 1925 in the Alpine style *(Shaanxi Nanlu 39–45)* (133 D3) (*ⓜ J7*) and the *Cité Bourgogne* built in 1930 *(Jianguo Xilu/corner Shaanxi Nanlu)* (133 D6) (*ⓜ J9*) as well as the *Shang-fang Garden*, preserving the Spanish or rational style *(Huaihai Zhonglu, Lane 1285)* (132 B4) (*ⓜ G8*).

Xinhua Lu, once a foreign lane lined with villas, invites you to take a walk beneath the trees in the northwest of the quarter. This street was used as the route for state visits because of its beauty, and Richard Nixon was driven along it in 1972. Today a number of trendy restaurants, bars and shops are to be found here and it is once more a highly desirable residential area. Colonial villas lie hidden in amongst the greenery: take a stroll through the enclave of the *Xinhua Villas*, laid out in the 1920s in a horseshoe *(Lane 211/329)* (0) (*ⓜ D8*) and wander through Lanes 115 and 119 to discover the longtangs and other beautiful architectural features, for who knows how much longer this will still be possible? *M1, M10 and bus 911 run on Huaihai Lu*

1 FUXING-PARK 复兴公园
(133 E4) (*K–L8*)

This park was laid out by the French in 1909 with a central lake, fountains, covered pavilions and flowerbeds. The early morning hustle and bustle here is a reason for getting up early: let the vibrancy of life wash over you and feel yourself filling with good humour! In the evening the park belongs to courting couples and the in-crowd who dance at the Guandii disco. *Entrances: Yandang Lu, Gaolan Lu, Fuxing Zhonglu | M1 Huangpi Road South*

2 FOUNDING PLACE OF THE COMMUNIST PARTY OF CHINA
中国共产党第一次全国
代表大会会址 **(133 F4)** (*L8*)

In an unimposing shikumen (stone gate house) 13 young Chinese met on 23 July 1921 to discuss the founding of a communist party. The conspiratorial meeting broke up because there was a traitor amongst the delegates – a member of the 'Green Band', an underground organisation that was later involved in the brutal suppression of the workers' uprising in 1927. Photos and documents of the founding members can be seen and a reconstructed scene of the conference. *Daily 9am–5pm | admission free | Xingye Lu 兴业路 76 | M1 Huangpi Road South*

3 MORRIS FAMILY ESTATE 瑞金宾馆 **(133 D5)** (*J8*)

The Morris family's villas, built from 1920, are to be found scattered across *Ruijin Park*. Their patriarch was the proprietor of the 'North China Daily News', once the largest English-speaking newspaper in China. The family also owned the *Canidrome*, a dog-racing track opposite the park's rear entrance. The races attracted up to 50,000 spectators and many of

Traditional mental exercise in the fresh air: men playing go in Fuxing Park

them lost the shirts off their backs here. The communists banned the 'decadent' pastime. The estate's main building was used to provide luxury accommodation for VIPs such as Madame Mao and is now used as a hotel. You can't go round it, but you can cast a glimpse into the hotel lobby. Chinese newly weds adorn the park on nice days, having their photograph taken against the romantic backdrop. *Ruijin Erlu* 瑞金二路 *118*

▣ SONG QINGLING'S RESIDENCE 宋 庆龄故居 (0) (*⑪ F8*)

It is said of the three rich and beautiful Song sisters: 'One loved money, the other power and the third her country'. The last one was Qingling. She married the 30-year-old revolutionary Sun Yat-sen in secret in 1915. The oldest sister, Ailing, chose the country's richest man, the banker H. H. Kung. Meiling, the middle sister, came to enjoy power as the wife of the Nationalist leader Chiang Kai-shek and died in 2003 in New York at the grand old age of 105.

Song Qingling, whose life can be followed by means of photos and interesting documents in the exhibition building on the estate, continued her husband's work after his death. She was highly revered by the communists and was the deputy State President from 1959 until 1975; she died in 1981. In 1948 Chiang Kai-shek presented her with this pretty villa, built in 1920 by a German shipping magnate, which you can now visit in its original condition. The state coaches in the garage and the garden with 100-year-old camphor trees are also worth see-

RELAX & ENJOY

How do you cope with the hustle and bustle of life in a big city? Well, by treating your body to the relaxation it needs! Beginners can start with a reflexology massage. Whilst your feet rest in a hot bath and your shoulders are massaged, you can use sign language to tell your masseur where your shoe has been pressing. Take note that the pressure point massage betrays your weak points, for example disturbed sleep, stomach ache, the start of a cold but, if the masseur 's good, he can sort all of that out. The best *shifu* (masters) are usually blind, which is why the *Blindmen Massage* is so popular – for the whole body, of course in the *Ganzhi Blinding Health Chamber (Yuyuan Lu 28, Nähe Tongren Lu) (132 C1) (⑪ H5)* or in the *Double Rainbow (Yongjia Lu 45)* (133 D5) (⑪ J8). Foreigners like to chill out in the Zen ambience of *Green Massage (e.g. Taicang Lu 58 |www.green-massage.com.cn)* (133 F4) (⑪ L8) where the massage eases aches and pains by relieving muscle spasm and helps speed up the body's natural healing processes. Very popular amongst the Shanghainese is the chain ● *Congen Massage Healthcare Club (e.g. Dagu Lu 436, near Shimen Yilu | www.shkangjun. cn)* (133 E2) (⑪ K6) where experienced *shifu* practise. The interior – black wood, burgundy walls and golden nick-nacks– isn't to everyone's taste but the prices are very reasonable, a one-hour foot massage costing approx. 90 Yuan. You can pay twice that in expensive salons but the treatment's available for about 30 Yuan in more modest shops.

ing. *Daily 9am–4.30pm | admission 20 Yuan | Huaihai Zhong-lu* 淮海中路 *1843 | M10 Shanghai Library*

5 SUN YAT-SEN'S RESIDENCE
孙中山故居 (133 E4) (*🕮 K8*)

By means of lots of photos and because it's been restored to its original state, the house provides you with an insight into the life and work of the man who is revered as the father of his country. Sun Yat-sen (1866–1925) was the leader of the revolutionary movement, which in 1911 sealed the end of the feudal empire. The political visionary proclaimed the republic in 1912, but just a short time later was ousted from the office of president. From 1918 to 1924 he lived with his young, beautiful wife Song Qingling in the French Concession. *Daily 9am–5pm | admission 20 Yuan | Xiangshan Lu* 香山路 *7*

6 RUSSIAN ORTHODOX MISSION CHURCH 东正教堂
(132 C3) (*🕮 J7*)

Built in 1934 to cater for the huge influx of Russian worshippers, the church is, with its sky-blue onion domes, one of the most beautiful examples of Russian culture in Shanghai. It's to be used as a church again after attempts to use the sacred halls as a stock exchange and then as a nightclub both ended in failure. The only success has been the Grape restaurant to the side of the church, with good and reasonably priced Shanghai cuisine. *Xinle Lu* 新乐路 *55 | M1 -Shanxi Road South*

7 SHANGHAI ARTS & CRAFTS MUSEUM 上海工艺美术博物馆
(132 C4) (*🕮 H8*)

A relic from colonial times and a curious venue for the promotion of socialist art in modern Shanghai: the 'White House',

as the Shanghainese call the French Renaissance-style mansion with its grand flights of steps, takes visitors back to the

A villa full of works of art:
Shanghai Arts & Crafts Museum

'golden age'. The building was erected in 1905 for the chairman of the French City Council. Chen Yi, the first mayor of Shanghai, lived here from 1950–54; there's a monument to him on the Bund. Today you can watch artists at work here, assuming they've not all just knocked off for their midday nap. You can admire and, if you wish, also buy skilfully worked embroideries and mildly scurrilous works of art such as root woodcarvings and internally painted perfume bottles. *Daily 9am–4pm | admission 8 Yuan | Fen-yang Lu* 汾阳路 *79 | M1, M7 Changshu Road*

8 SHIKUMEN OPEN HOUSE MUSEUM 屋里厢石库门博物馆

(133 F4) (*Ⓜ L8*)

The small but rather fine museum in a shikumen (stone gate) house gives a graphic insight into the life of a bourgeois family in the first half of the 20th century, and you can see a dwelling lovingly equipped with furniture and everyday objects. Have a look in the tiny, wedge-shaped *tingzijian* room on the landing, which was once rented out to impecunious writers and others. The longtangs (alley) houses, so typical of Shanghai, are illustrated by means of photos and drawings, and the redevelopment and reconstruction of the trendy Xintiandi district is also explained. You can get refreshments in a quiet tearoom. *Sun–Thu 10.30am–10.30pm, Fri, Sat 11am–11pm | admission 20 Yuan | Taicang Lu Lane 181 No. 25 太仓路 181 弄 25号 | M 1 Huangpi Road South*

AROUND PEOPLE'S SQUARE

人民广场

The British and American International Settlement was in the area behind the Bund, which is now the city district of Huangpu.

The International Settlement, measuring 14 sq mi, was bounded to the north by Suzhou Creek and to the east stretched beyond it – extending along the Huangpu. On ★ *People's Square* horses once used to gallop across the race track but, after gambling and horse racing were banned by the communist government, part of the race course became People's Square, which included a large avenue and spectator stands for use during parades. Today the modern city of Shanghai showcases itself here with its newly created centre. People come here on Sundays to feed the pigeons and fly kites. The opera house, by the French architect Jean-Marie Charpentier, is a real eye-catcher: the *Grand Theatre* (1998) combines a glass cube with a curved roof pointing heavenwards and in the evening is illuminated in all its glory.

The sight of the austere hulk of the municipal government building next door is rather sobering, but then your view settles on a space station, beamed down as it were by Captain Kirk. This futuristic complex (1999), the ☆ *Urban Planning Exhibition Hall*, reveals its visionary explosive force inside. By contrast, the Chinese teams of architects who designed the *Shanghai Museum* drew their inspiration from ancient times and the building (1995), modelled on an ancient bronze pot, houses a first-class collection of ancient Chinese art.

You'll find modern art in the northwest corner of the square in the former racecourse clubhouse (1928) with clock tower and Tuscan columns, which is now the *Art Museum*. Behind, towering up into the sky is the 284-m (932-ft) high *Tomorrow Square* (133 F2) *(∅ L6)*, which was erected in 2002 and, with its slender base and pointy tip, looks ominously like a rocket.

Park Hotel (No. 170, corner Huanghe Lu) (134 A2) *(∅ M6)*, a few steps further down Nanjing Lu, is almost dwarfed next to this: Shanghai's first skyscraper, built in 1934 and inspired by the American Radiator Building, was 84m (276ft) in height and until the 1980s the city's tallest building. It was designed by the architect Ladislaus Hudec (1893–1958), responsible in the 1920s and 1930s for the design of some of the most important buildings in Shanghai – including, diagonally opposite, the former Methodist church, now the *Mu'en Church* (134 B2) *(∅ M6)*, which you can reach through the People's Park. In the park **INSIDER TIP** *Starbucks (Nanjing Xilu 189)* (134 A2) *(∅ M6)* is waiting with a relaxing view of the surrounding greenery and you can sit on the quiet terrace or enjoy the view of the skyscrapers from the 🌿 roof garden at your leisure.

Then as now, *Nanjing Lu* was the city's main shopping thoroughfare. The *Department Store No. 1 (No. 830)* (134 B2) *(∅ M5)* stands as an old and famous temple to consumerism at the crossroads with Xizang Lu (Tibet Road), marking the beginning of the pedestrian zone. Its simple brick facade dating from 1934 stands in expressive contrast to the brilliance of the building opposite: *the 21st century Shimao International Plaza* (333m/1,093ft). In Shanghai the columns of commerce rise inexorably into the heavens, but in the faceless modernity of Nanjing Lu you can still find some beautiful old buildings such

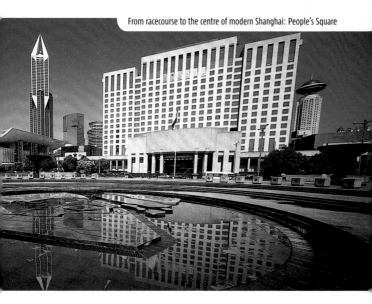
From racecourse to the centre of modern Shanghai: People's Square

as the *Yong'an* department store built in 1919 *(No. 635, corner Zhejiang Lu)* (134 B2) *(ᴍ N6)*. In the evening the neon advertising signs provide lots of photogenic colour.

In *Fuzhou Lu* you'll find bookstores, stationers and art accessories shops; it's the street of culture. In pre-communist Shanghai prostitutes would stand here beneath the red streetlights, and the street was lined with casinos and opium dens. At the crossroads with Jiangxi Zhonglu you can't miss the twin buildings of the *Metropole Hotel* and *Hamilton House*, which were designed in the 1930s by Palmer & Turner. The buildings, with entrances set in concave front facades, took on this design feature from the *Shanghai Municipal Council Building*

dating from 1919 and, with a commercial building on the fourth corner, create a circular square. *M2 Nanjing Road East*

■ ART MUSEUM 上海美术馆
(134 A2–3) *(ᴍ M6)*

The witty bronze figures outside the former racecourse clubhouse whet your appetite to see the art museum's collection. Even if the display of exhibits isn't exactly inspirational, you can see an interesting cross section of modern and contemporary Chinese art. One room is dedicated to the Shanghai School of traditional Chinese art. The museum also hosts the Shanghai Biennale, considered one of the city's most important cultural events, as well as regularly changing exhibitions of national and international

Living faith in the ultramodern city: ceremony in the Jade Buddha Temple

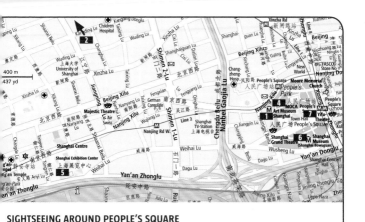

SIGHTSEEING AROUND PEOPLE'S SQUARE

1 Art Museum

2 Jade Buddha Temple

3 Jing'an Temple

4 MoCa Shanghai

5 Shanghai Exhibition Center

6 Shanghai Museum

7 Urban Planning Exhibition Hall

artists. *Daily 9am–5pm (entrance until 4pm) | admission free | Nanjing Xilu 南京西路 325 | www.sh-artmuseum.org.cn | M1, M2, M8 People's Square*

2 JADE BUDDHA TEMPLE 玉佛寺 ★
(0) (⟁ J3)

Shanghai's most visited Buddha sanctuary isn't exactly very old, but it's well preserved, full of religious life and richly adorned with statues, two of which – the most beautiful – gave it its name and were there from the very beginning of its foundation. In about 1880, a Chinese monk brought the Jade Buddhas from Burma together with the money donated by Chinese expatriates for the building of a temple. That first temple soon fell into disrepair and the present one was built in its place from 1918–28.

The entrance hall is directly on the street and opposite a splendid screen wall. During the Cultural Revolution images of Mao were stuck over the wings of the door to prevent the temple's destruction

because that would have meant the Red Guards having to tear Mao to get in. The laughing Buddha with his potbelly sits in the middle of the hall (which you can only enter from the rear), and on the sides the awe-inspiring heavenly kings threaten every kind of evil and remind visitors of the need for cleansing. Their attributes are snake and shield (west side) or pipa (Chinese lute) and sword (east side). Weituo, the Guardian of Learning, keeps watch on the inside of the temple behind the Buddha.

There's an incense burner on the other side of a courtyard and from there you come to the main hall, the roof of which is decorated with portrayals of the departure and return home of the Buddhist monk Xuanzang (7th century). Inside sit the Three Priceless Buddhas, from the left: Bhaisajyaguru, the Medicine Buddha, Shakyamuni (Gautama) and Amitabha, the Buddha of Infinite Light. On the sides there's a row of 20 so-called devas, divine protectors. On the other side you can see Guanyin, the Goddess of Mercy, riding over the sea on the giant turtle; above Gautama Buddha is to be seen meditating under the Bodhi tree, and below and next to the Guanyin the 18 holy monks (Luohan) are portrayed.

On the upper floor of the next hall, sitting in a shrine, is the larger of the two Burmese Jade Buddhas, an altogether delightful portrayal of the Shakyamuni. On the ground floor of the adjacent building to the west, the smaller Buddha is displayed in a reclining position along with a newer and larger, similarly prone Buddha from Singapore. Both show Buddha Gautama attaining nirvana. Also, have a good look at the elegantly turned wooden Guanyin figure, an approx. 400-year-old antiquity that stands rather in the shadow of the Jade Buddha. Go towards the exit and you'll discover in the side hall off the first courtyard yet another large bronze Buddha just as old. If you want to enjoy a real experience of what the religious life is like, then come when there's a INSIDER**TIP** full or new moon: the 1st and the 15th of the lunar month are traditional dates for religious celebrations and sacrifices to the gods, the Buddhas and Bodhisattvas. *Daily 6am–5pm | admission 20 Yuan, Jade Buddhas 10 Yuan | Anyuan Lu* 安远路 170

■3 JING'AN TEMPLE 静安寺 (132 B1)
(🕮 H6)

The 'Temple of Peace and Tranquillity', built in AD 247, was converted for use as a plastics factory during the Cultural Revolution and in the 21st century was permanently given a concrete rendering, artfully decorated with wooden carvings and luxuriantly gilded. Monks playing drums walk in a procession with the faithful in tow, their ears to their mobile phones, in a show of active contemplation of 'made in Shanghai'. *Daily 7.30am–5pm | admission 10 Yuan (free at full and new moon) | Nanjing Xilu* 南京西路 *1686 | M2 Jing'an Temple*

■4 MOCA SHANGHAI
上海当代艺术馆 (134 A2)
(🕮 M6)

The MoCA (Museum of Contemporary Art) displays contemporary art and modern Chinese design in an international context. In the not exactly cheap Italian ☙ INSIDER**TIP** *MoCA Caffée* on the roof of the small, sparkling glass palace you can escape from the madding crowd and, in peace and quiet, enjoy the view of People's Square. *Daily 10am–9.30pm | admission 20 Yuan | Nanjing Xilu* 南京西路 *231 | in the People's Park* 人民公园 | *www.mocashanghai.org | M1, M2, M8 People's Square*

■5 SHANGHAI EXHIBITION CENTER
上海展览中心 (132 C2) (🕮 J6)

This showy building dating from 1955 in Stalinist gingerbread style was intended to cement Chinese-Russian friendship, which fell apart just a few years later however. The red star now shines out over well-attended property fairs. If there are lots of black limousines parked outside the entrance in Nanjing Lu, this means the People's Congress is in session. *Nanjing Xilu* 南京西路 *1333 | M2 Jing'an Temple*

■6 SHANGHAI MUSEUM 上海博物馆
★ ● (134 A3) (🕮 M6–7)

Currently China's best museum for classical Chinese art, this is a genuine highlight, exhibiting one star turn after another: wonderful exhibits, outstanding presentation (with English descriptions) and an informative audio guide. The museum was founded in 1952, the present building opening in 1996.

An absolute must are the galleries of an-

A feast for the eyes: the finest porcelain in the Shanghai Museum

cient Chinese Bronze (1st floor), Ceramics and Porcelain (2nd floor) and Jades (4th floor). The Porcelain and Jade galleries contain not only first-class pieces – quite enchanting: **INSIDER TIP** ancient Jades – but also graphically present the changes in style and taste over the millennia. Then you need to go up to the 3rd floor with its watercolours and calligraphy. You should also have a look at sculptures, seals and art of the 'national minorities', furniture and coins as well as the frequently changing special exhibitions. You can have a rest in a tearoom on the 1st floor and a special delight is the very well stocked museum shop with outstanding replicas and the best art book section in the whole of China. *Daily 9am–5pm (Entrance till 4pm) | admission free, but number of visitors limited, so get here early and be prepared for long queues! | audio guide 40 Yuan (on deposit of passport or 400 Yuan) | Renmin Dadao* 人民大道 *201 | www.shanghaimuseum.net | M1, M2 People's Square*

7 URBAN PLANNING EXHIBITION HALL 城市规划展示馆 *(134 A3)* *(ɱ M6)*

After visiting the futuristic, six-storey Urban Planning Museum there's no longer any doubt about it: Shanghai is working towards becoming the world's greatest metropolis. It's a shame about the frilly curtains on the upper floor! But auspicious models show the city's building plans up to 2020. Hi-tech propaganda glorifies, and may perhaps even inhibit, the master plan for the future. And an enormous model of the city shows every new high-rise building and every new street, enabling residents to see how their district will one day be transformed into something beautiful. Alongside the model is a small theatre housing a 360° screen, and a video gives an impression of flying through the Shanghai of the future. Photos bear witness to the old times, documented in a museum in the basement. *Tue–Thu 9am–5pm, Fri–Sun 9am–6pm | admission 30 Yuan, special*

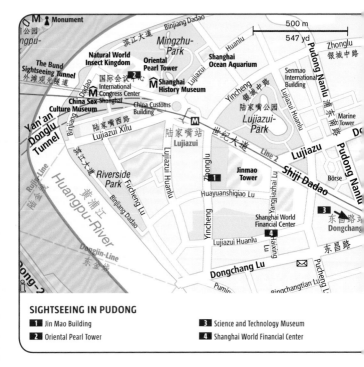

SIGHTSEEING IN PUDONG

1 Jin Mao Building

2 Oriental Pearl Tower

3 Science and Technology Museum

4 Shanghai World Financial Center

exhibitions extra | Renmin Dadao 人民 大道 *100 | www.supec.org | M1, M2, M8 People's Square*

PUDONG

浦东

The Huangpu River divides Shanghai into Puxi to the west and Pudong to the east. At the beginning of the 1990s farmers were still standing here working in their paddy fields.

Where storage sheds, dilapidated harbour facilities and decrepit apartment blocks were once an affront to the eye, today skyscrapers soar into the sky, and marble, glass and steel sparkle in the sun. More than 10,000 foreign firms have established a base here, whether in the free trade port of Waigaoqiao (0) (ⓜ *0*) or in the financial district of Lujiazui whose new stock exchange is reminiscent of the Grande Arche de la Défense in Paris.

Century Park (0) (ⓜ *0*), the largest park in the city and a place where you can hire tandem bicycles or cycling-cars, and broad streets like *Century Avenue (Shiji Dadao)* (135 F3–4) (ⓜ *Q–S 6–9*) emulate American examples. But the World Expo 2010 Site between the Nanpu and Lupu Bridges shows off some visionary ideas for urban planning which are very people and environment friendly: a wonderful ode to progress, to a future in cities that are both highly developed and worth living in. *M2 Century Park*

◼1 JIN MAO BUILDING 金茂大厦
★ ⚘ (135 F4) (Q7)

The jewel amongst the glass and steel palaces draws on the traditional design elements of a Chinese pagoda. Elegantly and airily divided, on its 88 floors it accommodates not only offices but one of the highest situated hotels in the world. On the 56th floor the building opens up inside to reveal a stunning barrel-vaulted atrium extending upwards to the 87th floor. The 421-m (1,381-ft) high tower was designed by the American team Skidmore, Owing & Merrill and is considered to be an outstanding example of a successful symbiosis of western and oriental architecture.

Instead of spending 88 Yuan to visit the viewing platform on the 88th floor, you can also enjoy the yz buffet lunch in the Grand Café (approx. 250 Yuan | tel. 021 50 47 12 34 87 78) on the 54th floor or a drink in the Cloud 9 bar on the 87th floor. *Century Avenue (Shiji Dadao)* 世纪大道 88 | M2 Lujiazui

◼2 ORIENTAL PEARL TOWER
东方明珠塔 ★ ⚘
(135 F3) (∅ Q6)

The kitschy but beautiful symbol of the city: rosy like the future is hoped to be and in the evening illuminated in a kaleidoscope of colours. The pearls symbolise purity – a pious wish in a country plagued by corruption. The 468-m (1,535-ft) high TV Tower provides observation decks (350m/1,148ft) and at a height of 259m (850ft) there's a INSIDER TIP new glass corridor round the central pearl from which those with a good head for heights can look all the way down. In the base of the TV Tower the city's history is graphically portrayed. *Daily 8.30am–9.30pm | admission 150 Yuan (up to the top) | Century Avenue (Shiji Dadao)* 世纪大道 1 | M2 Lujiazui

Pagoda with 88 floors: the 421-m high Jin Mao Building

Lots of exciting discoveries await you in the Science and Technology Museum

⑶ SCIENCE AND TECHNOLOGY MUSEUM 上海科技馆 (0) (0 0)

The impressive glass facade of the Science and Technology Museum rises up outside the entrance to Century Park. It features more than 14 interactive multimedia exhibits and experiments, which appeal both to children and adults. Amongst the attractions are the room with physical experiments and the tropical greenhouse with striking models of giant insects. Cinema visits (3D cinema and IMAX) cost extra. *Tue–Sun 9am–5.15pm (entrance until 3.30pm) | admission 60 Yuan | Century Avenue (Shiji Dadao)* 世纪大道 *2000 | www.sstm.org.cn | M2 Science and Technology Museum*

⑷ SHANGHAI WORLD FINANCIAL CENTER 上海环球金融中心 ☼ (135 F4) (0 Q7)

A 492-m (1,614-ft) high 'bottle opener', as it's known, has towered above the Jin Mao Building by 71m since 2008: the Shanghai World Financial Center, with 101 floors, the second highest building in China, is a Japanese investment and the work of the New York architects Kohn Pedersen Fox Associates.

Originally a round hole was intended to embellish the top of the building. But the Chinese were not at all impressed by this design, reminding them of the rising sun in the Japanese flag (which, they suspected, the constructors wanted to raise over Pudong). The hole now has the form of a trapezoid aperture, as a tribute to the harmony of nations. An observation deck at the top and a visit to the observatory are truly exhilarating – if you have a head for heights! *Daily 8am–11pm (entrance until 10pm) | admission 100–150 Yuan (94th–100th floor) | Century Avenue (Shiji Dadao)* 世纪大道 *100 | www.swfc-observatory.com | M2 Lujiazui*

IN OTHER QUARTERS

LONGHUA TEMPLE 龙华寺 ★ (0) (🚗 0)
Arguably the most beautiful temple in Shanghai, in front of its main gate stands a graceful pagoda dating from 1977. The temple was probably founded in the 3rd century AD, rebuilt in the 15th and 19th centuries and renovated in 2003. It was closed during the Cultural Revolution and sadly none of the statues that originally adorned it survived the destructive rage of the Red Guards.

Nevertheless the ‹Lustre of the Dragon Temple› has managed to preserve its tranquil charm. The repetitive singing of the monks to the sounds of the wood fish drums once more fills the air. At about 11.30am every day they walk in prayer through the five halls before they have lunch.

In the wing to the right you can also fortify yourself at this time with an excellent vegetarian INSIDER TIP noodle soup *(7.30–3.30pm | 10 Yuan)*. Then for 50 Yuan you can climb up to the top of the bell tower that dates from 1764, and strike the bell, which, as Buddhists believe, will relieve you from all your cares and woes.

BOOKS & FILMS

▶ **Empire of the Sun** – J.G. Ballard's highly acclaimed and prize-wining novel (1984) gives a graphic and moving account of his internment in a Japanese POW camp in Shanghai. It was also turned into a film by Steven Spielberg (1987).

▶ **Shanghai Architecture** – A comprehensive guide (2007). The author Anne Warr also offers guided tours *(www. walkshanghai.com)*.

▶ **New Shanghai Cuisine** – Jeremy Leung's visually stunning book makes a significant contribution to an understanding of the complex cuisine of Shanghai, exploring its rich culinary heritage through photographs and a lively narrative (2011).

▶ **When We Were Orphans** – Kazuo Ishiguro's prize-winning novel deals with a young man who returns to Shanghai in the 1930s to try to find his parents who suddenly disappeared when he was a young boy in the early 1900s (2000).

▶ **Death of a Red Heroine** – Qui Ziolong's novel, written in English, is more than an exciting whodunit; it also explores the tensions between old and new, socialist and capitalist which are central to Shanghai's ongoing development (2000).

▶ **The Painted Veil** – The film portrays the fraught relationship between a bacteriologist and a vain socialite against the backdrop of Shanghai in the 1920s and a cholera epidemic in rural China that he is sent to investigate (2006).

▶ **In Search of Old Shanghai** – Pan Ling's short non-fiction book is ideal to carry round as you seek out the landmarks it mentions, and it's full of useful and interesting information about Shanghai in its heyday (1986).

The *Jen Dow Vegetarian Restaurant (tel. 021 64 57 22 99)* in the rear section of the temple has been elegantly renovated and provides an incredibly substantial midday buffet lunch for approx. 140 Yuan or buffet dinner for about 160 Yuan. Visitors entering the restaurant **INSIDER TIP** from the *Longhua Lu 2787* can then go into the temple for free.

The adjacent ● *Lingua Park of Revolutionary Martyrs* with the *Memorial Museum (Park daily 6am–4.30pm, Museum Tue–Sun 9am–4pm | admission free)* provides the ideological contrast to the temple. Sculptures in the socialist realism style and a futuristic pyramid-shaped mausoleum are reminders of the victims of the massacre of 1927: Chiang Kai-shek's troops carried out a slaughter with the support of Shanghai's business and underworld, to which an estimated 5,000 striking workers and communists fell victim. The Communist Party then fled the city and began to seek power not by mobilising the industrial proletariat, but with the support of the farmers – which finally led to success.

Longhua Temple daily 7am–4.30pm | admission 10Yuan | Longhua Lu 龙华路 *2853 | M3 Longcao Road*

LU XUN PARK 鲁迅公园 ●
(131 F1) (*Ω P–Q1)*

Chinese people meet between six and seven in the morning in the park to practise t'ai chi ch'uan (a martial art) or mulanji (gymnastics with swords) and to dance the tango to music from their cassette recorders. Ad-hoc choirs belt out folk songs and later in the day pensioners hang wooden cages with song birds in the trees and bow their heads over board games. It was once a shooting range, but in the intervening 100 years many changes have been made and a lake, mountain and, in 1999, Hongkou Football Stadium have been added.

Lu Xun (1881–1936), modern China's most influential writer, spent the last years of his life in Shanghai and is buried in this park. The well-designed *Lu Xun Museum (Daily 9am–4pm | admission free)* – with a small bookshop where you can buy an edition of every book Lu Xun wrote, most in English – gives an insight into his life and work. In a small cinema **INSIDER TIP** one of Lu Xun's masterful prose poems is performed: you can listen to the melody of the Chinese language and with English subtitles admire his verbal imagery. Nearby there's also Lu Xun's House *(Daily 9am–4pm | admission 8 Yuan | Shanyin Lu 9, Lane 132 | to the southeast of the park)* (131 F2) (*Ω P–Q1)*.

If you head south from the main entrance (south gate), you'll come to the pedestrianised *Duolun Lu* (131 F2–3) (*Ω P2)*. The bronze sculptures in this street depict the writers of social criticism who in the first half of the 19th century created modern Chinese literature. Small shops with antiques, handicrafts and all sorts of curiosities invite you to rummage around. You simply must visit the *Doland Museum*

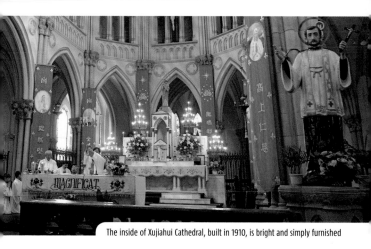

The inside of Xujiahui Cathedral, built in 1910, is bright and simply furnished

of Modern Art *(No. 27 | Tue–Sun 10am–6pm | admission 10 Yuan | Duolun Lu 27 | www.duolunmoma.org). You can take a break in the lovely* **INSIDER TIP** ▶ *Eucalyptus Café of the old-fashioned Koala Garden House (No. 240). Park admission free | M3, M8 Hongkou Football Stadium*

OHEL MOISHE SYNAGOGUE
犹太难民纪念馆 (0) (*ᗡ* S5)

Lying in the heart of the Jewish ghetto, the Russian Ashkenazi Jewish community built this synagogue in 1927. It houses a remarkable exhibition of photos, which serve as a reminder of what the Jewish ghetto was like in the 1940s. With the photographer Dvir Bar-Gal, you can take **INSIDER TIP** a walk in the footsteps of Jewish former residents *(half-day tours in English or Hebrew daily from 9.30am | 400 Yuan | mobile 1 30 02 14 67 02 | www.shanghai-jews. com). Mon–Fri 9am–4.30pm | admission 50 Yuan | Chang-yang Lu* 长阳路 *62 | near Zoushan Lu | M4, M13 Dalian Road*

SHANGHAI ZOO 上海动物园 (0) (*ᗡ* 0)
Pandas look so cute when they're devouring bamboo! Even if the way the animals are kept is not ideal (there are some 600 species on display), by Chinese standards this is a good zoo. Get to know the world of local animals and plants and enjoy the Chinese park design. There is one surprising view after another: classic pavilions, graceful bridges and lakes with pelicans paddling and ducks swimming. There's an enchanting atmosphere in spring when the cherry trees are in blossom, the green meadows are covered with loving couples, extended families enjoy a picnic and exuberant school groups romp around. *Daily 7am–4.30pm (last admission) | admission 40 Yuan, children under 1.20m free | Hongqiao Lu* 虹桥路 *2381 | M10 Shanghai Zoo*

XUJIAHUI CATHEDRAL
徐家汇天主堂 (0) (*ᗡ* E10)

The largest Catholic church in the Far East was built in 1910 in French Gothic style and it is testimony to the Jesuits' missionary activities. It's dedicated to the patron St Ignatius. The brick building with two bell towers has beautiful gargoyles and the inside is bright and simply furnished. *Sun 1–4pm | Puxi Lu 158* 蒲西路 *| M 1, M 9 Xujiahui*

Xu Guangqi's tomb and memorial lie near the cathedral in the park of the same name *(Tue–Sun 9am–4pm | Nandan Lu 16)* (0) *(🕮 D10)*. The Chinese scholar (1562–1633), honoured with a large stone bust, was a pupil of the Jesuit missionary Matteo Ricci (1552–1610) and led the reform of the Chinese calendar, the first collaboration between scientists from Europe and the Far East.

OUTSIDE THE CITY

ZHUJIAJIAO 朱家角镇 (141 D4) *(🕮 0)* Zhujiajiao on the banks of Dianshan Lake is the only one of the many water villages in the surrounding area that still belongs to Shanghai. The tide of renovation has also reached here but actually not until the present century. In Zhujiajiao restorations have been carried out carefully and far less has been destroyed compared with elsewhere. That's why in this little water town it's still possible to find the old, picturesque China in the narrow streets and along the many small canals. The history of the settlement began some 1,700 years ago and even today two-storey houses with pitched roofs from the Ming and Qing dynasties (1368–1911) line the canals, which are spanned by 20 old bridges.

When you've wound your way through the narrow streets lined with shops and admired the colourful wares, the view from the stone *Fangsheng Bridge* (Setting Fish Free Bridge) will provide a

KEEP FIT!

The best place for jogging in Shanghai is in Pudong: *Century Park (M 2 Century Park)* (0) *(🕮 0)* is a landscape park measuring about half a square mile which, thanks to the entry price of 10 Yuan, is not overrun by people just in search of relaxation. The running course, 4–6km/1.5–2.3mi long depending on the route chosen, takes you through meadows of flowers, small woods and past lakes and rivers.

If you'd rather take to the ice, then go to the *Mercedes-Benz-Arena* **(137 E5)** *(🕮 M13)*: the hall in Pudong built for the World Expo houses not only one of the largest concert arenas, with 18,000 seats, and a smaller venue, The Muse Mixing Room, used for live music events, numerous shops and restaurants, but also the best ice rink in the city. The *Century Star Skating Club (Daily 10am–10pm | admission for 2 hrs incl. skate hire Mon–Fri 50 Yuan, at weekends 60 Yuan | Shibo Dadao | M8 Zhoujiadu)* boasts outstanding facilities. Beginners can book individual tuition for 30 minutes for 120 Yuan.

Kung Fu, subdivided into several schools, has been made popular in the west by the film stars Bruce Lee and Jackie Chan. So why not try it out whilst you're in the home of this martial art? You can do so in the *Mingwu International Kungfu Club (Hongmei Lu 3212, Hongchun Building 3/Fl | tel. 021 64 65 98 06 | www.mingwukungfu.com | M10 Longxi Road)* (0) *(🕮 0)*. They offer wushu, t'ai chi ch'uan (shadow boxing), qigong exercises, jeet kune do and, if you're really cool, karate.

A trip to the water village Zhujiajiao transports you into a world of bridges and small canals

moment's calm and you can relax watching the rusty barges slowly gliding past. Old women have small live fish for sale, so grab one (but be careful, they're slippery!) and throw it back into the water, which is an old Buddhist custom said to bring good fortune. The bridge, taking its name from this tradition, is supported on five stone arches. It's 72m (236ft) long and 7.40m (24ft) high and is the largest and most beautiful bridge of this type in the Yangtze delta. Even if the 'gondolieri' don't sing here, there's still romance to be found on a trip through the canals on a wooden barge.

The water town has been thoroughly developed for tourists. The entrance fee, payable at the city gate by the car park, entitles you to visit the sights that are marked on the map. These include the *Kezhi Garden* with a magnificent five-storey building, the Moon View Pavilion, and the equally impressive City God Temple with its bloodthirsty paintings. Also,

don't miss the exhibition of 1,000-year-old ceramic and jade finds from the delta: you'll be amazed at the artistry and the aesthetic sensitivities of ancient China. Another exhibition tells of rice cultivation and the subsequent processing of the country's most important staple food. The exhibits in the small *Fishery Museum* are also very graphically presented.

If you get to the ☀ *Granny Teahouse* you've at last finished up in the best place in the village as far as the views are concerned, and you can fortify yourself here for the return journey.

Admission 30, 60 or 80 Yuan (depending on sight/boat trip) | full day tours by tourist bus from Shanghai Stadium (O) (🗺 E12) or one-hour journey on the Hu Zhu express bus (6am–10pm every 20–60 min) from south of People's Square at the crossroads with Pu'an Lu/ Yan'an Donglu (134 A4) (🗺 M7) or M9 to Sheshan (141 E4) (🗺 O) plus taxi | approx. 40km/25mi from Shanghai

FOOD & DRINK

Going out for a meal is one of the greatest attractions in Shanghai because it's here, in the nation's melting pot, that you can enjoy specialities from almost every province in China.

In the cold north, cooking is simple and rich in calories and garlic. It's not just the horse people of the steppe who have made their distinctive mark on Beijing cooking, but also the imperial cooks who created the world famous Peking duck. In the warm south, food is prepared really light and fine so that many people regard Cantonese cooking as the best in the country – one speciality being *dim sum*, stuffed pastry. In the west, cooking is sharp: in Szechuan there's a preference for pepper and red chilli and people like to gather round the cooking pot to enjoy a sort of fondue.

The Shanghai culinary repertoire is traditionally based around rice, fish and seafood and all sorts of freshwater fish from the water-rich interior. There's chicken and duck as well, of course. Food is prepared with lots of oil, soy sauce and rice wine, often served with a sweet and sour sauce. Because winters can be penetratingly cold, food is not only rich in calories but must also warm from within, which is why thick sauces are prepared and there's a lot of coating with breadcrumbs and deep frying, and meals tend to be rounded off with a warm soup.

Green tea is served as a refreshing, slightly bitter drink. In the summer and autumn *xigua* (freshly squeezed melon juice) is preferred to lemonade. Of course there are also lots of alcoholic drinks: the light

Shanghai has become a delight for food lovers: Chinese and international dishes compete for the public's favour

Tsingtao beer is brewed locally in Qingdao and is a dark beer, unlike most local beers which are pale lagers. Chinese wine is also not bad at all, Ningxia wines having beaten Bordeaux in tastings in December 2011. And the Maotai liqueur, with its exceptionally pure mellow soy sauce flavour, is not to be underestimated.

A Chinese restaurateur will serve up everything the kitchen has to offer in order to impress you with his generosity. Several courses are always dished up at a banquet and rice, by the way, is only served at the end of the meal. If you eat everything to show how much you've enjoyed the meal, it'll be understood in China as a sign that you've not had enough, so always remember to leave a morsel or two on the side of your plate. It's the custom always to offer a toast before drinking and, after making the toast, the host will encourage his guest to drain his glass with a shout of *ganbei*. But he will then continue to make sure that your glass is never empty, but constantly full to the brim. So just stop drinking before you fall off your chair! And in China it's always down to just one person to pay the bill: if you've not been invited, as a rich foreigner you'll be expected pay.

If you've ever seen how the Chinese ce-

the slightest doubt, don't touch the food even if you've already ordered it. In general it's always wise to be careful with anything deep fried. Make sure that fresh oil is being used. You can usually

Refreshing and sociable: green tea in a traditional ambience

lebrate eating in a really exuberant way, then you'll be a firm believer in the victory of the great proletarian revolution. At the very least, as far as 'bourgeois' table manners are concerned, these seem to have been eradicated. People slurp, smack their lips and burp, and the table is in no time transformed into a pile of rubbish. In China the meat is not separated from the bone in the kitchen, but chopped up and served in bite-sized pieces together with bone, skin and gristle. The Chinese then sort it all out in their mouth, which leads of course to lots of food being spat out.

If you're eating outside in the street, then trust your senses of taste and smell: what smells good and tastes good is also usually absolutely fine to eat. If you have

eat boiled, baked or steamed food without too many concerns as long as it's not already been kept warm for a long time.

In Shanghai you can eat remarkably well for very little money. Prices are ridiculously cheap in the local pubs and, in comparison with big cities in the west, the best restaurants aren't expensive either. Lots of pubs also offer very reasonable lunch menus, making it worthwhile to eat at midday!

The Chinese like to eat early: lunch is served from 11am till 2pm, dinner from 5 till 9pm at the latest. Western pubs stay open longer, and in the restaurant miles you can get a bite to eat at any time. When a phone number is given below, this means a table reservation is essential.

RESTAURANT MILES

HENGSHAN LU 衡山路
(132 A–B 4–5) (∅ E–G 8–9)
Here and in the side streets you'll find restaurants catering for western tastes and trendy bars where there's lots going on in the early evening. *M1 Heng-shan Road*

INSIDER TIP ▶ JIASHAN MARKET
嘉善坊 (132 C5) (∅ J9)
Shanghai's first 'Urban Garden Community' has been set up in an old knitwear factory, hidden away in a narrow street. It's a green oasis with a focus on an environmentally friendly lifestyle. Bars furnished with natural materials are grouped round a quiet courtyard. In the *Melange Oasis* café/restaurant not only will you find refreshing fruit juices and light Mediterranean-style food made from local organic produce, but you can also enjoy a thoroughly delightful experience. *Shanxi Nanlu* 陕西南路 *25–37 Lane* 弄 *550 | South of the Shaoxing Lu crossroads, turn right at second pedestrian crossing into the street leading to Jiashan Lu | www.*

jiashanmarket.com | M1, M10 Shanxi Road -South, M9 Jiashan Road

SUPER BRAND MALL 正大广场 ⚡
(135 E3) (∅ P6)
The biggest shopping centre in China is where Pudong's hungry office workers go to eat in lots of restaurants and cafés. Various price categories, some with self service. The bars with a balcony and view of the Bund are particularly nice. *Lujiazui Xilu* 陆家嘴西路 *168 | M2 Lujiazui*

YUNNAN LU 云南路
(134 B3–4) (∅ M6–7)
This is a street lined with one bar after another. What you'll find here is good traditional cooking, local colour and the fact that you can get something good to eat even if you don't understand a word. *M1, M2 People's Square, M8 Dashijie*

ZHAPU LU 乍浦路 (135 D1) (∅ P4–5)
Suzhou Creek is where the mile-long stretch of brightly lit fish restaurants begins. In the *Dynasty Restaurant (no. 324 |*

MARCO POLO HIGHLIGHTS

CAFÉS & TEAHOUSES

Moderate) there is more than a guarantee of freshness: your fish is only caught when you've chosen your meal from the fish tanks. *M10, M12 Tian-tong Road*

CAFÉS & TEAHOUSES

INSIDER TIP CITIZEN CAFÉ
(133 D3) *(𝄞 J7)*

This small but charming café and bar is a haven of peace and quiet in the shopping area full of clothes shops around Huaihai Lu. *Jinxian Lu* 进贤路 *222 | www.citizen-shanghai.com | M1, M12 Shanxi Road South*

OLD CHINA HAND READING ROOM
汉源书店 **(133 D5)** *(𝄞 J9)*

Unique mix of library, local history museum and café. Deke Erh is not only the proprietor but also a photographer and her illustrated books are a stimulus for you to do more exploring. *Shaoxing Lu* 绍兴路 *27 | M9, M12 Dapuqiao*

INSIDER TIP OLD SHANGHAI TEAHOUSE
老上海茶馆 𝄢 **(134 C5)** *(𝄞 O8)*

The teahouse with its old-fashioned interior is reminiscent of Shanghai in the 1930s. You can enjoy sipping tea in peace and

GOURMET RESTAURANTS

100 Century Avenue 世纪 100
★ ● 𝄢 **(135 F4)** *(𝄞 Q7)*

The avant-garde Park Hyatt Restaurant in the Shanghai World Financial Center stands out by virtue of its excellent western, Chinese and Japanese cuisine, pleasant service and a stunningly beautiful view which you can also enjoy over a cappuccino. Menu from approx. 400 Yuan. *Park Hyatt* 柏悦酒店, *91–93/F | Century Avenue (Shiji Dadao)* 世纪大道 *100 | tel. 021 38 55 14 28 | shanghai. park.hyatt.com | M2 Lujiazui*

Jean Georges 𝄢 **(135 D3)** *(𝄞 O6)*

Haute cuisine created by Jean-Georges Vongerichten with a slight Asian twist is served in an atmosphere of dark, stylish elegance. It's particularly lovely in the evening when the lights of the skyline illuminate the dining room. Menu approx. 570 Yuan. In the Nougatine a three-course menu is served daily 6–7pm for approx. 230 Yuan. No need to book . *Three on the Bund, 4/F | Zhongshan Dong Yilu* 中山东一路 *3 |*

tel. 021 63 21 77 33 | www.threeonthe bund.com

Mr. & Mrs. Bund 𝄢 **(135 D2)** *(𝄞 O6)*

Masterchef Paul Pairet is famous for his intelligent French cuisine. You can enjoy the most tender fillet steak and the most heavenly lemon tart in a relaxed atmosphere but one with a certain panache. The wine list includes 32 wines by the glass. Menu about 400 Yuan, business lunch (Mon–Fri 11.30am–2pm from approx. 2,200 Yuan. *Zhong-shan Dong Yilu* 中山东一路 *18, 6/F | tel. 021 63 23 98 98 | www.mmbund.com*

Stiller's ★ 𝄢 **(139 E2)** *(𝄞 P9)*

The chef Stefan Stiller works his magic in the Cool Docks by the Huangpu. His restaurant is a modestly styled refuge for people who want to enjoy themselves and don't need to dazzle. Menu approx. 400 Yuan. *Zhongshan Nanlu* 中山南路 *505, Bldg. 3, 6–7/F | tel. 021 61 52 65 01 | www.stillers-restaurant.cn/ wordpress | M9 Xiaonanmen*

quiet and, from the windows on the first floor, also observe the hustle and bustle in Old China Street (Fangbang Lu). *Fangbang Zhonglu* 方浜中路 *385 | M10 Yu Garden*

DI SHUI DONG 滴水洞
(133 D3) (*⑪ K7*)
The authentic Hunan cuisine offers great value for money and is pleasantly served

Refuge in the style of the 1930s: immerse yourself in the atmosphere in the Old Shanghai Teahouse

VIENNA CAFÉ G (133 D5) (*⑪ J9*)
This café in the French Concession is where you can enjoy homemade Viennese patisseries, but it is also a cosy place for Sunday brunch with organic bread, served from 10am till 2pm. And on Thursday evenings films are shown, ranging from European Indie to Oscar nominated films, INSIDER TIP and they're free. *Shaoxing Lu 25, Building 2* 绍兴路25弄2号 *| M9, M12 Dapuqiao | www.viennashanghai.com*

CHINESE FOOD

BI FENG TANG 避风塘
(133 E3) (*⑪ J7*)
A traditional restaurant chain - witty decor (don't be surprised to see boats!) and good, reasonably priced food. The shrimp dumplings are delicious, as is the roast duck soup. You can get something to eat INSIDER TIP here 24/7. *Changle Lu* 长乐路 *175 | M1, M10 Shanxi Road South | Budget*

in a rustic ambience. For something both truly delicious and unforgettable, try the soup with lotus seeds. *Maoming Nanlu* 茂名南路 *56, 2/F | M1, M10 Shanxi Road -South | Budget*

1221 THE DINING ROOM 餐馆1221
(0) (*⑪ G8*)
You can enjoy light, classy and highly praised Shanghai cuisine in a simple, cultivated ambience. *Yan'an Xilu* 延安西路 *1221 | Near Panyu Lu, in a small street | Tel. 021 62 13 65 85 | M3, M4 Yan'an Road West | Moderate*

GUYI 古意湘味浓
(132 C2) (*⑪ H6*)
Fiery Hunan cuisine. Cumin-crusted ribs (ziran paigu) are their signature dish and, like all their food, will make you work up a sweat. Just be careful you don't burn your tongue! *Fumin Lu* 富民路 *89 | Budget*

LOCAL SPECIALITIES

▶ **ba bao ya** – roast duck, filled with the 'eight treasures' (e.g. lotus seeds, dried dates, ham, chicken, rice, green beans, bamboo, carrot, cucumber) (photo right)

▶ **baozi** – steamed dumplings filled with meat or, as caide baozi , with a vegetable filling, often eaten for breakfast

▶ **dazhaxie** – hairy crab from Yangcheng Lake west of Shanghai, only available from September to the start of December. Aficionados use eight tools to tease out each dainty morsel

▶ **doufu** – tofu or bean curd: very rich in protein, dried, deep fried or cooked in soy sauce. Very fiery as mapo doufu (with minced meat), very much an acquired taste as chou doufu ('stinky tofu')

▶ **gongbao jiding** – a wonderful mix of diced chicken with bright red chillis and golden peanuts with a sweet and sour sauce

▶ **hongshao rou** – belly pork or beef, cooked in black soy sauce and ginger, garlic, chilli peppers and rice wine and served with hard boiled eggs , potatoes and vegetables

▶ **jiaohuazi ji** – 'beggar's chicken' is a whole chicken first wrapped in lotus leaves, then packed in clay and stewed in its own juices on an open fire

▶ **jiaozi** – long dumplings filled with meat, spring onions and vegetables. They are cooked or boiled and at the table dipped in a small bowl of vinegar, soy sauce and chilli

▶ **mantou** – steamed buns made of yeast dough and neutral in taste, popularly eaten for breakfast

▶ **songshu guiyu** – sweet and sour mandarin fish (fresh water fish) with pine nuts

▶ **suanni helan dou** – snow peas with sweet Cantonese sausage and garlic

▶ **xiaolong bao** – small dumplings filled with pork or prawns. You catch the delicious hot stock with a soup spoon (photo left)

▶ **xiazi dawushen** – braised sea cucumber with shrimp roe

▶ **yandu xiantang** – soup with fresh bamboo and two types of meat

JUJUBE TREE – VEGETARIAN LIFESTYLE
枣子树 ★ ☺
'We are concerned for the earth, the animals and your health' – this is a lifestyle with ever more adherents. But it's also worth a visit because the crispy roast mushrooms, taro rolls in pumpkin sauce, sesame pancakes and bamboo shoots

juice are all really delicious here! The reasonably priced *set lunch* (about 30 Yuan) means it's very busy. *Fengxian Lu* 奉贤路 *258* | *tel. 021 62 15 75 66* | *M2, M12 Nanjing Road West* (**133 D1**) (*㊉ K5*); *Songshan Lu* 嵩山路 *77 (In the rear courtyard on the left)* | *tel. 021 63 84 80 00* | *M1 Huangpi Road -South* (**134 A4**) (*㊉ M7*) | *www.jujubetree.com* | *Budget*

LOST HEAVEN 花马天堂 ★ (0) (㊉ F7)
Specialities from the southwest Chinese province of Yunnan, inspired by the local ethnic groups' cuisine. Their art decorates the restaurant and the intimate *Mask* bar. Try the 'Dai style chicken with seven spices'. The location on the Bund is also to be recommended for the good cocktails (Happy hour daily 5–7pm). *Gao-you Lu* 高邮路 *38 Between Fuxing Lu and Hunan Lu)* | *tel. 021 64 33 51 26* | *M1, M7 Changshu Road; on the Bund: Yan'an Donglu 17 (Near Si-chuan Nanlu)* | *tel. 021 63 30 09 67* (**135 D3**) (*㊉ O7*) | *www.lostheaven.com.cn* | *Moderate*

MEI LONG ZHEN 梅龙镇酒家 (133 D1) (㊉ K6)
Authentically Chinese: carvings, golden dragons, lanterns. The food is perhaps a bit oily, but that's just genuine *Shanghainese,* as is this traditional restaurant in an old city palace. *Nanjing Xilu* 南京西路 *Lane* 弄 *1081 no. 22* | *Rear courtyard, near Jiangning Lu* | *tel. 021 62 53 53 53* | *M2, M12 Nanjing Road West* | *Moderate*

NANXIANG STEAMED BUNS RESTAURANT 南翔馒头店 ★ (135 D5) (㊉ O8)
Famous dim sum restaurant with a gallery by the pond outside the Yu Yuan, recognisable from the long queues at the takeaway counter on the street. The dining rooms, always full, are on the three upper floors and, as you ascend, the pri-

Ultramodern but a delight: People 6

ce goes up, the wait goes down and the food gets better and better. On the 2nd floor you can enjoy the famous xiaolongbao for just 15 Yuan. *Yuyuan Laolu* 豫园老路 *85* | *tel. 021 63 55 42 06* | *Budget*

PEOPLE 6 穷六人间
The door doesn't open until you've put your hand into the jaws of a metal sculpture. A luminescent frosted glass staircase takes you up to the galleries on the 1st and 2nd floors. A hi-tech lift delivers the food which is better than you might have expected in such an ultramodern style of restaurant. In the *People 7* branch you're given the door code when you book. *People 6: Yueyang Lu* 岳阳路 *150* | *tel. 021 64 66 05 05* | *M1 Hengshan Road* (**132 B5**) (*㊉ H6*); *People 7* 萤七人间: *Julu Lu* 巨鹿路 *805* | *tel. 021 54 04 07 07* (**132 C2**) (*㊉ J6*) | *Moderate*

PIN CHUAN SICHUAN CUISINE (132 B4) (㊉ H8)
Sharply spiced Sichuan cuisine is served in a black, white and red ambience. The 'chicken from the village with sea snail' and the tofu with shrimps are highly recommended. Lovers of chilli will be in heaven here without having to put their

hands too deeply into their pockets. *Taojiang Lu* 桃江路 *47 | tel. 021 64 37 93 61 | M1, M7 Changshu Road | www.pinchuanchina.com | Moderate*

Crispy vegetables in the Yè Shanghai

SEAGULL SIGHTSEEING RESTAURANT
海鸥饭店 ⚓ (135 E2) (⚹ P5)
Behind the Seagull Hotel you climb up to the terrace by the river from where you can enjoy a splendid view of the city and the ocean steamers and rust buckets on the Huangpu. *Huang-pu Lu* 黄埔路 *60 | Budget*

INSIDER TIP WORKSHOP NO. 9 车间
(0) (⚹ E12)
You can eat here like the working masses in Mao's times: in a canteen, with enamel tableware and the waiters dressed in work clothes. *By the bus terminal near gate 7 | Tianyaoqiao Lu* 天钥桥路 *666 | tel. 021 64 26 67 67 | M4 Shanghai Stadium | Budget*

INSIDER TIP XIANG ZHANG GARDEN 香樟花园时尚厨房 ● (132 B4) (⚹ G8)
Shanghai cuisine with a refined ambience: there's comfortable seating in the modern building with a view through the tall panes

of glass to the busy Hengshan Lu. Try the *soy pork with sticky rice* and *Thai Pomelo salad! Hengshan Lu* 衡山路 *2 | tel. 021 64 33 43 85 | M1 Hengshan Lu | Moderate*

YÈ SHANGHAI 夜上海 ★ ●
(134 A5) (⚹ L8)
Inventive Shanghai cuisine with a view of the cobbled streets, and upstairs it's open and modern. Recommendations include stewed prawns in chilli sauce, deep fried fillet of beef with mushrooms and goose liver. *Huangpi Nanlu* 黄陂南路 *338 | Xintiandi* 新天地 *| tel. 021 63 11 23 23 | M1 Huangpi Road -South | Moderate*

THE YONGFOO ÉLITE 雍福会
(132 A4) (⚹ G8)
Once the British consulate in Shanghai, the villa is a now a restaurant paying homage to Shanghai's cosmopolitan culture in its glory days at the beginning of the 20th century: dark mahogany, old leather and Chinese porcelain are resplendent in the light of the candelabra. This is traditional Shanghai cuisine and a really nice place for a nostalgic cup of tea with a view of the garden. *Yongfu Lu* 永福路 *200 | tel. 021 54 66 27 27 | www.yongfooelite.com | Expensive*

INDIAN KITCHEN 印度小厨 (0) (⚹ 0)
Here you can enjoy fresh cucumber salad, fragrant curry and crispy naan bread at reasonable prices. The tender tandoori chicken and curry mutton with coconut milk are highly recommended. *Minsheng Lu* 民生路 *480 (Near Zhangyang Lu) | M2 Dongchang Road | Budget*

KATHLEEN'S 5 ⚓ (134 A2) (⚹ M6)
Enjoy continental food with a view of People's Square: on the roof terrace, the former racecourse clubhouse clock tower

tells you when it's time to interrupt your meal for a visit to the Grand Theatre next door. You can then discuss the performance whilst you tuck into your dessert. Lunch Mon–Fri from 140 Yuan. *Art Museum* 上海美术馆 | *Nanjing Xilu* 南京西路 *325 | tel. 021 63 27 22 21 | www.kathleens5.com.cn | M1, M2, M8 People's Square* | *Moderate*

INSIDER TIP **ORIGIN** ☺ (133 E6) (*∭ K9*)
Enjoy fresh salad sitting on a small balcony, excellent organic food, friendly service in quiet rooms set in the lively, trendy district. *Jianguo Zhonglu* 建国中路 *155 | Also accessible via Tai-kang Lu* 泰康路 *274 | www.originsh.com | tel. 021 51 72 13 00 | M9, M12 Dapuqiao* | *Moderate*

LARIS

This is one of the most sophisticated restaurants in Shanghai, known for its fish – try the pan-fried red snapper – and for being one of the few places to serve quality raw seafood, so you can feast on delicious oysters and clams. 3 Zhong Shan Dong Yi Lu Near Guangdong Lu | *tel. 021 63 21 99 22* (132 E4) (*∭ H8*); | *www.threeonthebund.com* | *Expensive*

SHINTORI NULL II 新都里无二
(132 C2) (*∭ H6*)

An amazing place to eat - bamboo trees, very high ceilings and clean, light walls and a minimalist interior design. The Japanese food is outstanding - try the grilled cod: it's melt-in-your-mouth delicious – and the presentation is excellent. *Julu Lu* 巨鹿路 *803 (lack of a number at the entrance, follow the bamboo path) | tel. 021 54 04 52 52 | M2, M7 Jing'an Temple* | *Expensive*

SIMPLY THAI 天泰餐厅

With glorious colours and minimal design, the restaurant is a great attraction with the aromas of Thai cuisine. The coconut and mushroom soup, chicken and lemon grass are divinely sharp. *Dongping Lu* 东平路 *5 C | tel. 021 64 45 95 51* (132 B4) (*∭ H8*); *Madang Lu* 马当路/Corner Xingye Lu 兴业路 (Xintiandi 新天地) | tel. 021 63 26 20 88 (133 F4) (*∭ L8*) | www.simplythai-sh.com* | *Moderate*

INSIDER TIP **WAGAS** ☺ (132 C3) (*∭ H7*)
The local chain in Puxi and Pudong feeds the city's cosmopolitan health-conscious in-crowd: with delicious wraps and sandwiches, French croissants, excellent coffee and cool smoothies. Enjoy the relaxed atmosphere and the simple but comfortable décor. *Donghu Lu* 东湖路 *7 | M1, M10, M12 Shanxi Road South* | *Moderate*

LOW BUDGET

▶ In *The Grandma's* you can enjoy outstanding Hangzhou dishes, very generous portions beautifully presented and absurdly cheap. It's worth waiting for a table because here you can feel completely full for approx. 30 Yuan! *Xizang Beilu 166, Joy City 8/F | M8, M13 Qufu Lu* (0) (*∭ M4*)

▶ La Casbah is a nice, small Moroccan pizza, pasta and sandwich shop (about 30 Yuan each). Good cappuccino and delicious cheese cake. *Huaihai Zhonglu 155 | M10 Shanghai Library* (132 A4) (*∭ G8*)

▶ Really lovely and delicious: at *Simply Thai* you can eat Mondays from 5 to 7pm for half price. From 60 Yuan per person, reservation needed before 5pm.

SHOPPING

CITY **WHERE TO START?**
The worldwide luxury brands have taken up residence in the colonial buildings on the **Bund**. Here and in the luxury department store Plaza 66 in the western **Nanjing Lu** shoppers will not know which way to turn when faced with the quality goods on display. The prices in the shops in the posh **Xintiandi** district are also very high. This is where the tourists often flock to, as well as the trendy **Taikang Lu** or the **Yuyuan Bazaar** which specialises in traditional souvenirs. You can get bargains at the clothes and fabrics markets and in the **Hongqiao International Pearl City** if you're good at haggling.

'Made in China' is a guarantee for kitsch which has now acquired almost cult status. Shanghai is a shopping paradise for all those who like shopping cheap and quick. But, with increasing purchasing power, a new market for top class products is also being built up here. Chinese manufacturers are increasingly producing top quality products with surprisingly innovative design with the result that 'Made in China' is developing into a seal of quality. Whilst imported luxury goods are more expensive than in Europe, it's worth buying Chinese goods in the middle and upper price ranges, especially sportswear and sports items. You can get hold of handmade clothing and handicraft items such as jewellery, embroidery and carvings for very reasonable prices and fulfil your

Spending spree in the megacity: everything you don't actually need – and lots you've always dreamt of

dreams of cashmere, silk and pearls. Taking a relaxed stroll through the narrow streets off Taikang Lu and discovering a small but distinctive present is a real pleasure. An outstanding address for serious souvenir hunting is the Hongqiao International Pearl City department store, with clothes and golf gear on the 1st floor, pearls on the 2nd and carpets and luggage on the 3rd, and the atmosphere is relaxed and you can bargain, though sorting through the goods takes some time. If you'd rather avoid fighting your

way through crowds of shoppers, then you should avoid going to the Yuyuan Bazaar and the clothes markets at the weekend. It's a lot calmer and quieter in the fashionable Xintiandi district and, even if you don't buy anything here, you should at least go and look at the beautiful items in the shop windows!

As a rule the prices in the major department stores are reasonable. In department stores and supermarkets the prices are even more reasonable, but at markets and in ordinary shops you should be prepared to haggle, usually by offering 40% to 50% of the stated price before settling on 60% to 70%. In the Yuyuan Bazaar you can even talk them down to 30% of the figure first quoted. Always check the items for faults before buying. At the markets the rule is 'bought as seen'. When haggling it's always

street. *Dongtai Lu* 东台路/*Corner Liuhe-kou Lu* 浏河口路 | *M8 Laoximen*

FANGBANG LU ANTIQUES MARKET
方浜路藏宝楼 (134 C5) (*ω N8*)
In this four-storey building you'll find numerous junk dealers peddling their

The biggest shopping temple in China: the Super Brand Mall in Pudong

a good idea to have the price of a similar item in mind. Always remain friendly and never show too much interest in an item. As soon as the trader accepts your offer, the deal is then done. So never state a price which you're not prepared to pay. But always bear in mind that not every trader is offering his products at ridiculously inflated prices. And if someone's offering self-made trinkets for just a few Yuan, then you shouldn't try to haggle.

You can shop every day from 8 or 10am till 9 or 10pm. State-run shops usually close as early as 6pm.

wares. On the top floor hawkers from the outlying areas come, though weekends only, **INSIDER TIP** to lay out their treasures. If you get here early, know how to spot a fake and can really haggle, you can snap up a real bargain. *Fangbang Zhonglu* 方浜中路 *457 | M10 Yu Garden*

BOOKS

FOREIGN LANGUAGES BOOKSTORE
外文书店 (134 C3) (*ω N6*)
The book shop stocks a good range of English books about China and Shanghai. *Fuzhou Lu* 福州路 *390*

ANTIQUES & BRIC-A-BRAC

DONGTAI LU ANTIQUES MARKET
东台路古玩市场 ★
(134 A5) (*ω M8*)
Here you'll find antique (though not necessarily authentic) ceramics, embroidery, wood carvings, clocks and watches, jade and Mao memorabilia in stalls along the

GARDEN BOOKS 韬奋西文书局
(133 D3) (*ω J7*)
The city's widest selection of books and novels about China and Shanghai, newspapers and magazines, café with delicious ice cream. *Changle Lu* 长乐路 *325 | www.gardenbooks.cn | M1, M10, M12 Shanxi Road South*

ELECTRICAL GOODS

HONGKONG PLAZA 香港广场
(133 F3) *(ᴍ L7)*
Department store with small shops stocking all the major electrical brands but also local ones at very reasonable prices. *Huaihai Zhonglu* 淮海中路 *282 | M1 Huangpi Road South*

GALLERIES

M 50 – MOGANSHAN LU
M 50 创意园 ★ ● **(0)** *(ᴍ K2)*
The new generation of artists has, like the old artisans, benefited from an excellent education but is very much more free-spirited, which has resulted in a burst of artistic energy which the whole world is now looking at in astonishment. The artists have found the place and freedom to experiment in old factories and warehouses on the Suzhou Creek. In the now well established artists' quarter there's a lot on offer which is, to be honest, little more than mediocre, so you're well advised to concentrate on the galleries *Eastlink (Bldg. 6, 5/F | www.eastlinkgallery.cn), Islands 6 (Bldg. 6, 2/F | www.islands6.org.), BizArt (Bldg. 7, 4/F | www.arthubasia.org)* and *Art Scene Warehouse (Bldg.4, 2/F | www.artscenewarehouse.com).* Most galleries open at 10am but are closed Mondays. You can fortify yourself with dumplings in the INSIDER TIP Bandu Cabin, *where, once a month on a Saturday, there are small live concerts (Block 11 | www.bandumusic.com). Moganshan Lu* 莫干山路 *50 | Near Changhua Lu | www.m50.com.cn*

SHANGHART GALLERY 香格纳画廊
(0) *(ᴍ K2)*
In 1996 the Swiss art connoisseur Lorenz Helbig became the first foreign gallery owner in Shanghai to exhibit – in very modest surroundings – modern Chinese art. He now lives in Moganshan Lu and his gallery is open every day from 10am to 6pm. *Moganshan Lu* 莫干山路 *50, Bldg. 16 and 18 | www.shanghartgallery.com*

DEPARTMENT STORES

You'll find large department stores with a wide range of Chinese and foreign goods on Nanjing Lu, one of the busiest shopping streets in the world, including the *Department Store No. 1 (No. 830 | M1, M2, M8 People's Square)* **(134 B2)** *(ᴍ M5)* or the luxurious *Plaza 66 (No. 1266 | M2 Nanjing Road West)* **(134 B2)** *(ᴍ J5)*, also on Huaihai Lu *(M1, Bus 911)* **(132–133 A–F 3–4)** *(ᴍ J–N7)* and at the Xujiahui *(M1)* **(0)** *(ᴍ E10)*.
In Pudong on the other side of the Huangpu River, you'll find the largest shopping centre in the country: the *Super Brand Mall (Lujiazui Xilu 168 | M2 Lujiazui)* **(135 E3)** *(ᴍ P6)*.

★ **Dongtai Lu antiques market**
The fascination of rummaging and bargaining → p. 68

★ **M 50 – Moganshan Lu**
New art in old factories and warehouses → p. 69

★ **Taikang Lu**
Finding that special gift in lovely little shops → p. 72

★ **Yuyuan Bazaar**
Silk scarves, dragons and gongs: the ultimate kick for shopaholics → p. 73

MARCO POLO HIGHLIGHTS

FRANGIPANI – NAIL BAR
(132 B4) (*∅ G8*)

Enjoy having your finger nails varnished in a nicely renovated old building with an easy-going ambience (from 105 Yuan). They have nail varnish in every colour of the rainbow. *Fuxing Xilu* 复兴西路 76 | *M1 Changshu Road*

Red brings good luck: beautifully coloured greetings cards in Fuzhou Lu

ART & CALLIGRAPHY ACCESSORIES

You can get all the materials and equipment you need for painting, drawing and calligraphy in *Fuzhou Lu* (134C3) (*∅ N6*). Try shop *no. 331* or the stationery shop *(no. 355), a* paradise for painters: **INSIDER TIP** the higher the floor, the more reasonable are the prices for paints and paint brushes.

FASHION & FABRICS

You can find trendy clothes in the boutiques around Huaihai Lu (133 D3–4) (*∅ J7–8*): in Shaanxi Nanlu, Nanchang Lu, Maoming Lu and Changle Lu. You'll find modern, authentic fashion design in *Xinle Lu.* There are also hot shops with fashion, artworks and bric-a-brac in *Jinxian Lu.* Why not get yourself a pinhole camera from *Lomography (No. 126)* and make a record of the spectacular Shanghai street fashion?

The *qipao,* the stylish and tight-fitting silk dress, also known as a Mandarin gown, and jackets in the style of the Tang dynasty are to be found in department stores, by the Yu Yuan or in *Maoming Nanlu (133 D3) (∅ J7)* (To the north of Nanchang Lu; from there bear left into Changle Lu, as far as Shaanxi Lu). The shops are expensive, but have really nice things and also offer a sewing and alteration service, e.g. *Changle Lu Lane 201 (M1, M10, M12 Shanxi Road South).*

FENSHINE FASHION ACCESSORIES PLAZA 淘宝城凤翔服饰礼品广场

Fake designer clothes, leather goods and watches are sold under the counter, as well as everything that's fashionable in China and silk goods and souvenirs. It's best to avoid the crowds at the weekend. And bargain hard - everything's fake and the asking prices are absurd! *Nanjing Xilu* 南京西路 *580 | M1, M2, M8 People's Square* (134 A2) (*∅ L6*) *and the underground market at the Science and Technology Museum metro station* (0) (*∅ 0*)

INSIDER TIP INSH (133 E6) (*∅ K9*)

The fashion label stands for *In Shanghai* and captures the esprit of the metropolis in graphically designed men's and women's T-shirts, brightly coloured clothes and accessories such as caps and handbags. The designer Helen Lee goes for modern, easily sold motifs, but also embroiders army coats with traditional colourful flowers and tailors bizarre dresses. *Taikang Lu* 泰康路 *Lane* 弄 *210 no. 3 International Artist Factory, 2/F; also Fumin Lu* 富民路 *172* (132 C3) (*∅ H7*) | www.insh.com.cn

MARY CHING (0) (*∅ F8*)

Whether it's skyscraper stilettos or leopard print wedges – the young shoe designer Alison Yeung makes enchantingly beautiful shoes – but unfortunately wickedly expensive. *Wukang Lu* 武康路 *374–376 (Near Hunan Lu)* | www.marychingshanghai.com | *M10 Shanghai Library*

STAR PLACE (132 C3) (*∅ J7*)

Here funky, colourful clothes hang on long poles – and don't cost much at all! *Xinle Lu* 新乐路 *66*

SHANGHAI TANG 上海滩

Chinese luxury label for classically elegant clothes, accessories and home interior design, unfortunately expensive. *Maoming Nanlu* 茂名南路 *59* (133 D3) (*∅ J7*) *and Taicang Lu* 太仓路 *Lane* 弄 *181 no. 15* | *Xintiandi* (134 A5) (*∅ L8*) | www.shanghaitang.com

FABRIC MARKET (139 D3) (*∅ O10*)

Here you'll find fabrics on three floors and very reasonable prices if you're good at haggling. Finished samples make it a lot easier to choose but check the fabrics carefully for faults before you buy. On the ground floor there are finished goods for sale. *Lujiabang Lu* 陆家浜路 *399/Nancang Lu* | *M4 Nanpu Bridge*

INSIDER TIP▶ YAMADO (133 E6) (*∅ K9*)

Hunting bags for Indians: Yamado makes pouches and bags from natural materials such as leather, pelt and feathers and his designs are marked by an apparently archaic quality. A dream, and not only for Pocahontas! *Taikang Lu* 泰康路 *252* | *M9, M12 Dapuqiao*

For musical souvenirs, you'll find specialist shops for musical instruments and good CD shops in *Fenyang Lu* (132 C4) (*∅ H8*) by the Conservatory of Music *(No. 8)*. The *Violin Shop (No. 9)* specialises in making fiddles.

Glasses and contact lenses are reasonably priced and are sold in numerous places.

LOW BUDGET

▶ *Decathlon Shanghai Factory Outlet Store:* a French manufacturer with an enormous range of functional clothes, sports and camping items – good quality at reasonable prices. *Yinxiao Lu 393 (0)* (*∅ 0*) | *Opposite M2, M7 Long-yang Road; also in the Xianxia Xilu 88 (0)* (*∅ 0*) | *M2 Beixinjing* | www.decathlon.com.cn

▶ Hand-made items costing next to nothing but not factory products: you'll find pretty jewellery such as filigree pearl necklaces in the *Hongqiao International Pearl City* and in the *Yuyuan Bazaar*. Hand-painted paper dragons make a nice present and don't weigh very much. From travelling hawkers you can get pendants artistically made from drinking straws which are said to bring good fortune and look wonderful as Christmas tree decorations.

The chains *Paris Miki* and *American Eyes* are to be found in department stores, e.g. in the *Grand Gateway* by the Xujiahui (0) (*⅏ E10*).

PEARLS & JADE

Jade and pearls are sold in the *Yuyuan Bazaar (134–135 C–D 4–5) (⅏ O7–8)*, for example in the jewellery store in *Fuyou Lu 288.*

HONGQIAO INTERNATIONAL PEARL CITY 虹桥国际珍珠城 (0) (⅏ O)

Precious, fashionable nicknacks and lots of souvenirs. You'll find a wide range of pearls on the 2nd floor and *Ling Ling (No. 2001)* and *Susie's Pearl & Jewelry (No. 2010)* are to be recommended. Diagonally opposite you can get something to eat and drink in *Hongmei Food Street. Hongmei Lu* 虹梅路 *3721/Corner Hongqiao Lu* 虹桥路 *| M10 Longxi Road*

SOUVENIRS

NEST 巢 😊 (133 E6) (⅏ K9)

Environmentally friendly and socially acceptable goods, made of natural, sustainable or recycled materials, which you can wear or use to decorate your house. In addition to bags, cups and tableware you'll also find here smart, timeless ladies' and children's fashions made from organically grown cotton: the creative label INSIDER TIP Finch works with a collective of artists and its 'Made in China' products are carbon neutral. *Taikang Lu* 泰康路 *Lane* 弄 *210 Bldg. 3, International Artist Factory, 2/F | M9 Dapuqiao*

TAIKANG LU 泰康路 ★ (133 E6) (⅏ K9)

Some years ago, artists, gallery owners and designers were the first to make the derelict buildings and factories here into their places of work and residence. Bohemian cafés and boutiques followed. The

Forget the latest trend, it's all about style: boutique in the trendy Xintiandi district

lanes 210, 248 and 274 today make up, under the name *Tianzifang,* one of the city's liveliest districts. You can rummage around in countless small shops in search of unusual small gifts. Galleries like the one owned by the well known Shanghai photographer Deke Erh *(Lane 210 no. 2)* sell desirable art and cultural objects. And if you fancy a break from your wandering about and want to sit down for a while, there are restaurants (e.g. *Origin, p. 65)* and cafés, such as the *Kommune Café (Lane 210 no. 7)* **INSIDER TIP** with the biggest cups of cocoa in the city. *M9, M12 Dapuqiao*

XINTIANDI 新天地 **(133 F4)** *(ΩΩ L8)*

There are exclusive shops with modern Asian designer goods in this trendy, affluent and pedestrian district. A lot of it is fake but some is very original and creative as in the *Shanghai Trio Boutique (Taicang Lu 181 | www.shanghaitrio.com).* At *Decoster Living (Xingye Lu Lane 123 no. 6, 2/F)* the traditional Chinese porcelain blue is given a new interpretation, being used to decorate home textiles, crockery and all sorts of utensils. And don't walk past the luxury fashions at *Shanghai Tang (see p. 71)* and *Annabel Lee (Taicang Lu Lane 181 no. 3)* without venturing a look inside. *M1 Huangpi Road South or M10, M13 Xintiandi*

URBAN TRIBE 城市山民 **(132 A4)** *(ΩΩ G7)*

Stone gray linen garments made only from natural fabrics and simple, but gorgeous hand-made jewellery, candles and earthenware pots are reminiscent of craft markets but with a strong emphasis on natural living. Amongst the upper class in Shanghai society, which has had enough of loud shades, garish colours, outlandish frills and fake gold glitter, it's now an exclusive trend to focus on the essential. The boutique's purist ambience is very impressive and it's also used as a

photo gallery, and there's **INSIDER TIP** a small, quiet tea garden serving exquisite tea. *Fuxing Xilu* 复兴西路 *133 | M10 Shanghai Library; also Taikang Lu* 泰康路 *Lane 248 no. 14* **(133 E6)** *(ΩΩ K9) | www. urbantribe.cn*

YUYUAN BAZAAR 豫园商业街 ★ ●
(134–135 C–D 4–5) *(ΩΩ O7–8)*

Around the City God Temple and the Yu Yuan you'll find the Old City's historic and vibrant shopping centre, giving those who really know how to haggle plenty of scope. There's kitsch and all sorts of junk in *Chenxiangge Lu* and the *Fumin Store (Fuyou Lu/corner Anren Jie).* In *Fangbang Lu* the trend is more in the direction of arts and crafts. The splendid mishmash will give you lots of pleasure but it's also likely to have quite an impact on your wallet! Enthusiastic souvenir hunters love the hustle and bustle in the alleys and the bargaining for silk scarves, jade jewellery, books bound in brocade and dragons made of wood, stone and paper. Men are particularly attracted to the clay pipes, flutes and gongs made from hammered metal, but make sure they don't add too much weight to your luggage. And will there be room left for antique embroidery, beautiful wood carvings or elegant tea sets from Fangbang Lu? *M10 Yu Garden*

INSIDER TIP ZEN LIFESTORE
钲家具艺廊 **(132 B5)** *(ΩΩ H8)*

Beautiful, functional, well crafted items by Chinese designers such as little wooden boxes, lamps, painted porcelain, fabric gifts, scented candles and fine fragrances. On the top floor there's a delightful café serving organically produced tea. *Dongping Lu* 东平路 *7 | M1 Changshu Road; also in the Xintiandi district: Xingye Lu* 兴业路 *118* **(133 F4)** *(ΩΩ L8) | M1 Huangpi Road - south or M10, M13 Xintiandi | www.zenlifestore.com*

ENTERTAINMENT

The **Cool Docks** is a place to see and be seen: a chilled beer by the fountain in the centre of the complex or a sundowner at the Sunny Beach can be the start of a long evening. You can also observe the crowds strolling past in the trendy **Xintiandi** district whilst enjoying a pick-me-up espresso at Starbucks or a cocktail outside the TSMK bar. If you fancy something a little more sophisticated, then you can chill out in the jacuzzi on the terrace of the Vue Bar on the **Bund**. And from there you can take in the spectacular view of the Huangpu and modern Pudong.

This city vibrates at night. And the only question is, 'Where shall we go?' To a bar for a beer? Or put in an appearance in a glamorous lounge on the Bund?

The scene in Shanghai is constantly changing, new bars opening in the blink of an eye and sometimes disappearing just as quickly. The magazine 'That's' and the websites *www.urbanatomy.com, www.cityweekend.com.cn* and *www.smartshanghai.com* all have their finger on the pulse of the nightlife.

Now that the cobbles in Maoming Lu, once the hottest street in the city, have cooled down, celebrations around Hengshan Lu and in Fuxing Park have become wilder and wilder. The bars in Julu Lu are well-known for the pretty girls with their routine smiles. And there are

Photo: Maoming Nanlu

This is where night becomes day: Shanghai's nightlife explodes like a firework – in a fascinating blaze of colour

more trendy pubs just round the corner in Changshu Lu, Huashan Lu and Wulu-muqi Lu. Things are a bit more sedate in Nanjing Xilu where networking after work in the *Long Bar* in the *Shanghai Centre (No. 1376)* is the done thing. Round the corner in *Malone's (Tongren Lu 255)* is the Americans' place of preference for relaxing and taking a break from their posting abroad. The Xintiandi bar and restaurant district is just the place to sit outside in the summer and observe the crowds strolling past.

A relaxed start to a pub crawl is in the Cool Docks *(Zhongshan Nanlu 505)* **(139 E1)** *(🗺 P9)* where you can enjoy a cocktail at the ● INSIDER TIP *Sunny Beach (Behind the docks by the Huang-pu | Entrance 20 Yuan)* and then go on to *Stiller's (p. 60)* restaurant to have a really good meal, though beer, burger and chicken wraps are more affordable at *Top Choice (No. 9 in the Cool Docks square, by the fountain)*.

It has to be said that Beijing is the centre for rock music, but there's been a jazz re-

Have a drink in the Glamour Bar and be captivated by the luxurious atmosphere of the 1930s

vival in the House of Blues and Jazz and in other clubs in Shanghai. In the clubs and discos it's predominantly a mix of mainstream rap, otherwise it's Disco, House and Rhythm and Blues that's to be heard. Internationally well-known rock groups, stars and DJs are drawn to Shanghai. And more and more theatres and concert halls are offering an impressive platform for artists from all over the world.

Going out for a night's fun and entertainment in Shanghai comes at a price. Expensive or trendy pubs such as Bar Rouge and Muse demand a *cover charge* per table and you have to eat 3,000 to 4,000 Yuan's worth if you want to settle there for the night. You also have to be prepared for queues, paying for admission and pretty lousy service in some places. But it's all worth it!

BARS, CLUBS, PUBS & LIVEMUSIC

BARBAROSSA LOUNGE ★
(134 A2) (*M M6*)
Exotic ambience in the People's Park: on balmy summer evenings this is a wonderful place to sit in a three-storey wooden palace looking down on the lake, enjoy Maghrebian dishes and puff away on your water pipe. *Sun–Thu 11 am–2am, Fri, Sat 11am–3am | Nanjing Xilu 南京西路 231 | In the People's Park 人民公园 | tel. 021 63 18 02 20 | M1, M2, M8 People's Square*

BAR ROUGE 〰 (135 D2) (*M O6*)
The most famous club in Shanghai, its Murano red glass chandeliers get the beautiful, the rich and the up-and-coming in the mood for champagne. Infatuated by the dolce vita, you look down from the terrace onto the dark river and see the barges and cutters chugging past. *Daily 6pm–1.30am | Zhongshan Dong Yilu 中山东一路 18, 7/F | www. bar-rouge-shanghai.com*

BLUE FROG 蓝蛙 (133 D4) (*M J8*)
Here you can enjoy a cool beer and delicious burgers from 11 in the morning till late into the night. The **INSIDER TIP** *Fire Cracker Pasta* will really perk you up! *Maoming Nanlu 茂名南路 207-6; also Super Brand Mall 正广场 (133 E3) (M P6) and Hongmei Entertainment Street 虹梅步行休闲街 (0) (M 0) | www.bluefrog.com.cn*

CLOUD 9 九重天
(135 F4) (*Q7*)
The 360-degree panoramic view in one of the highest lounges in the world – situated on the 87th floor! – is a real knock-out. The prices are outrageous and you need to book a table. *Daily from 5pm | Jin Mao Building, 87/F | Century Avenue (Shiji Dadao)* 世纪大道 *88 | tel. 021 50 49 12 34 | M2 Lu-jiazui*

INSIDER TIP **CONSTELLATION BAR**
(132 C3) (*J7*)
A small, quiet bar with carefully mixed drinks at not excessive prices, and the *Moscow Mule* can also be recommended. The sleek interior in the *Constellation II* is even more impressive. *Daily 7pm–2am | Xinle Lu* 新乐路 *86 | M2 Shanxi Road South; Constellation II: Yongjia Lu* 永嘉路 *33 | M10 Shanxi Road South* (133 D5) (*J8*)

COTTON'S 棉花 (132 A6) (*G9*)
Housed in a romantic villa in the French Concession, this is a restaurant and garden bar serving delicious pizzas! *Daily 11am–2am | Anting Lu* 安亭路 *132 | www.cottons-shanghai.com | M1 Hengshan Road*

EDDY'S 嘉依咖啡厅 (0) (*E8*)
A good gay bar, the first in the city opening in 1995, it attracts local and foreign customers aged 20 to 40. It's nicest early in the evening. *Daily 8pm–2am | Huaihai Zhonglu* 淮海中路 *1877 | near Tianping Lu | M10 Shanghai Library*

GLAMOUR BAR 魅力酒吧
(135 D3) (*O6*)
Old-fashioned 1930s' ambience, stupendous view, but note there's a dress code. This is a sumptuous place, the varied twists and turns of the bar inspired by a sexy high heel! In March the international Shanghai Literary Festival is held here with lectures in English. *Daily from 5pm | Guangdong Lu* 广东路 *5, 6/F | Corner Bund* 中山东一路 *| www.m-glamour.com | M2 Nanjing Road East*

MARCO POLO HIGHLIGHTS

★ **Barbarossa Lounge**
Wooden palace and water pipe: enjoy the exotic ambience in the summery People's Park → p. 76

★ **House of Blues and Jazz**
A Shanghai institution for good music and relaxed evenings → p. 78

★ **Yu Yin Tang**
Underground music made in China → p. 80

★ **Grand Theatre**
International guest performances in the Palace of Lights → p. 80

★ **Long Bar in the Waldorf Astoria**
Popular, comfortable and very solid – a bar with a focus on the essentials → p. 78

★ **Vue Bar**
Comfort with a view: let the day come to a splendid, but thoroughly relaxed conclusion → p. 79

★ **Shanghai Oriental Art Centre**
Stunning architecture and outstanding acoustics produce a musical feast for ears and eyes → p. 81

HOUSE OF BLUES AND JAZZ ★ 布鲁斯与爵士之屋 (135 D3) *(ɯ 06)*
This long-established Shanghai institution, now located just off the Bund, is one of the best (and smokiest) clubs in the city, with good music and lots of atmosphere. On the spacious first floor you can sit close to the band or more quietly towards the back. *Tue–Sun 7pm–2am, live music 9.30pm | Fuzhou Lu* 福州路 *60 | M2 Nanjing Road East*

good jazz, good whisky and good cigars. And today this is again a place to meet and to listen to good jazz. The young star trumpeter and cosmopolitan composer **INSIDERTIP** Theo Croker and his sextet play Nu Jazz (Tue–Sat 9.30pm–0.30am). Croker mixes the sound of the Mississippi with the tones of the Himalayas. Or you can listen to the veteran band giving new life to the jazz of the 1930s (daily 6.30pm–9.30pm). *Fairmont Peace Hotel* 和平饭店 *| Nanjing Donglu* 南京东路 *20 | M2 Nanjing Road East*

The Far East swings in the House of Blues and Jazz – and there's plenty of atmosphere

JADE ON 36 翡翠36酒吧 ☼ (135 E4) *(ɯ P7)*
Glamorous plush restaurant bar with a divine **INSIDERTIP** view of the Bund, which gets the heart beating faster. *Sun–Thu 5–10pm, Fri, Sat 5pm–2am | Fucheng Lu* 富城路 *33 | Tower 2 of the Pudong Shangri-La Hotel* 浦东香格里拉大酒店, *36/F | www.shangri-la.com | M2 Lujiazui*

JAZZ BAR IN THE PEACE HOTEL (135 D2) *(ɯ 06)*
In the times before and after Mao, this old-fashioned English bar was famous for

LONG BAR 廊吧
IN THE WALDORF ASTORIA ★ (135 D3) *(ɯ 07)*
The glittering, 34-m (112-ft) long mahogany bar is very masculine, very solid and very impressive, and the leather bar stools are very comfortable – and that's why this is a favourite meeting place throughout the day, and not only for old gentlemen. From 11am to 1pm you can feast on oysters, from 9.45pm till 0.30am there's live music. *Mon–Sat |*

Waldorf Astoria 华尔道夫大会所 | *Zhong-shan Dong Yilu* 中山东一路 2

NEW HEIGHTS 新视角 ● ☆
(135 D3) (*∅ O6*)

The bar is beautifully but unspectacularly furnished and boasts a wonderful view of the river and the Pudong skyline. If the Bar Rouge is too snobby for you, you can still enjoy the refined savoir vivre. *Daily 11.30am–1am | Zhongshan Dong Yilu* 中山东一路 *3, 7/F | Three on the Bund | www.threeonthebund.com*

O'MALLEY'S IRISH PUB 欧玛莉餐厅
(132 B4) (*∅ H8*)

Guinness garden and music pub and a place to play darts, watch sport and sit by the fire. *Mon–Sat 11am–1.30am, Sun 1pm–1am | Taojiang Lu* 桃江路 *42 | www.omalley-shanghai.com | M1, M7 Changshu Lu*

SASHA'S 萨莎 (132 B4) (*∅ G8*)

The villa was built in the 1920s by the powerful Song family and Chiang Kai-shek once lived here. Today it's a good place for people over 30 who want to drink a well cared for beer. Excellent in the summer, with a famous patio. *Sun–Thu 11am–1am, Fri, Sat 11am–2am | Dongping Lu* 东平路 *9*

VUE BAR 非常时髦 ★ ● ☆
(135 E1) (*∅ P5*)

A comfortable bar with terrace to chill out on, with your feet dangling in the cooling jacuzzi or, in winter, drawing up close to the warming fire. Fabulous views of the Bund and Pudong. When the weather's nice, you can make yourself comfortable on the loungers. *Daily 5pm–1am | Hyatt on the Bund, 32–33/F | Huangpu Lu* 黄浦路 *199*

DANCE CLUBS & DISCOS

INSIDER TIP M1NT ☆ (135 D3) (*∅ O6*)

Really popular and quite a fantastic club, this is where the so-called or self-styled elite of Shanghai come to party. When international star DJs come to Shanghai, this is where they come. Best cocktails, lovely roof terrace with fabulous views. *Mon–Sat from 6pm | Fuzhou Lu* 福州路 *318, 24/F | www.m1nt.com | M2 Nanjing Road East*

INSIDER TIP MURAL 摩砚
(132 A5) (*∅ G9*)

Cavernous setting with a medium-sized dance floor and a Buddhist flavour and

LOW BUDGET

▶ A good place to drop anchor is the ☆ *Captain's Bar*, the globetrotters' meeting place, where you can drink your fill quite reasonably and hold hands whilst admiring the view of the lights of Pudong. *Daily 11am–2am | Fuzhou Lu 37, 6/F | M 2 Nanjing Road East* (135 D3) (*∅ O6*)

▶ Celebrations as though in Mexico: in *Zapata's* the bar's open on Wednesday with 'free flow of magaritas for all the ladies' till midnight – people dance on the counter to music from the 1980s. *Daily from 5pm | Heng-shan Lu 5* (132 B4) (*∅ G8*)

▶ The *Shanghai Symphony Orchestra* showcases its expertise every Friday at 7.30pm in a rehearsal. *Entrance 20 Yuan | Hunan Lu 105 (Near Wu-kang Lu) | tel. 021 64 33 35 74 | www.sh-symphony.com | M10 Shanghai Library (0)* (*∅ F8*)

where everything's good: the music (Saturdays Latin live band), the drinks (*Kamikaze Shot*), the prices (Fridays open bar: 'All you can drink' for 100 Yuan), the clientele (young and colourful). *Daily 7pm–3am | Yongjia Lu 永嘉路 697 | www.muralbar.com | M1 Hengshan Lu*

MUSE 缪斯 (0) (ⓜ H4)
The New Factories is becoming the new evening hot spot and the Muse is considered to be the hottest club in the city. There's dancing on two floors: House upstairs and Hip Hop downstairs. *Daily 8.30pm–4.30am | Yuyao Lu 余姚路 68 (Near Haifang Lu) | www.museshanghai.cn | M7 Changping Road (south of Jing'an Temple)*

MUSE AT PARK 97 (133 E4) (ⓜ K8)
Part of the Muse empire, the two-storey dance club with a modern design in Fuxing Park has DJs who do absolutely fantastic mixes of Hip Hop, House and Electro Nights. *Daily 8pm–2am, Fri/Sat longer | Gaolan Lu 皋兰路 2a | www.muse-shanghai.cn/en-us*

PARAMOUNT 百乐门 (132 B1) (ⓜ G6)
Glittering Art Deco dance palace which was Shanghai's greatest night club in the 1930s. If you don't have a partner, for 300 Yuan for the evening you can hire a 'Taxi Dancer' to escort you across the floor dancing to live music. *Daily 1pm–4.30pm and 8.30pm–1am | Yuyuan Lu 愚园路 218 | M2 Jing'an Temple*

INSIDER TIP ▶ THE SHELTER (132 A4) (ⓜ G8)
Underground music in the air raid shelter: dark and loud, this is a great place for wild dancing. Local and international independent musicians and DJs play Reggae, IDM, Drum'n'Bass, Electro, Hip Hop.

The drinks are also very reasonable here. *Wed–Sat 7.30pm–2am | Yongfu Lu 永福路 5 (near Fuxing Lu) | M10 Shanghai Library*

YU YIN TANG 育音堂 ★ (0) (ⓜ C6)
Independent, Indie and Hardcore Rock: the collective who founded the alternative club are amongst the precursors of the underground music scene in China. Check the programme at *www.yuyintang.org*. Very decent prices. *Tue–Sun 9pm–2am | Kaixuan Lu 凯旋路 851 | behind the metro station | M3, M4 Yan'an West Road*

THEATRE, CONCERTS & ACROBATICS

Theatre and concert tickets are obtainable at the evening box office. Ticket prices start at 50–80 Yuan and can go as high as 600–1,680 Yuan. It's a good idea to get tickets in advance (This service is available in lots of hotels) or book online. Ticket and event information is available at *www.culture.sh.cn* or in the *Shanghai Cultural Information Centre (Fengxian Lu 272 | tel. 021 62 17 24 26 | M2 Nanjing Road West)* (133 E1) (ⓜ K5).

GRAND THEATRE 上海大剧院 ★ (134 A3) (ⓜ L–M6)
Concerts, operas and ballet: world famous ensembles make guest appearances in this beautiful showpiece on People's Square, designed by the French Architect Jean-Marie Charpentier. It comprises three theatres, the largest, the Lyric Theatre, holding 1,800 seats. *Renmin Dadao 人民大道 300 | tel. 021 63 86 86 86 | www.shgtheatre.com | M1, M2, M8 People's Square*

SHANGHAI CENTRE THEATRE 上海商城剧院 (132 C1) (ⓜ J5–6)
Look on in awe and amazement at trapeze artists and contortionists. This is

where the best acrobats in China show off their widely praised art, and the venue is evidence of Shanghai's increasing encouragement of the arts. *Daily 7.30pm | Entrance from 100 Yuan (ticket kiosk at the road entrance) | Nanjing Xilu* 南京西路 *1376 | ticket reservation tel. 021 62 79 86 63 | www.shanghaicentre.com*

SHANGHAI CONCERT HALL
上海音乐厅 **(134 A4)** *(𝄞 M7)*

The concert hall was re-opened in 2004 after the 1931 Art Deco building was relocated by 66m and renovated at a cost of 18 million US dollars. The acoustics are as wonderful as the music performed by the Shanghai Symphony Orchestra. *Tickets 9am–7.30pm | Yan'an Donglu* 延安东路 *523 | tel. 021 53 86 66 66 | www.shanghaiconcerthall.org | M1, M2, M8 People's Square*

INSIDER TIP ▶ SHANGHAI CULTURE SQUARE 上海文化广场
(133 D5) *(𝄞 J8)*

On the site of the former canidrome (dog racing track) which is now a green park, 'a phoenix spreading its wings' has settled, or at least that's the lovely image which inspired the architect. The ultramodern concert hall with more than 2,000 seats was, when it opened in 2011, the largest in the world. The underground stages host outstanding performances of world famous musicals. *Yongjia Lu* 永嘉路 *36 | M1, M12 Shanxi Road South*

SHANGHAI ORIENTAL ART CENTER
东方艺术中心 ★ **(0)** *(𝄞 0)*

An overpowering architectural masterpiece by the Frenchman Paul Andreu, ultramodern technology and superb acoustics define the context for world-class musical performances. *Tickets 9.30am–7.30pm | Dingxiang Lu* 丁香路 *425 | tel.*

Weightless bodies in the Shanghai Centre Theatre

021 68 54 12 34 | www.shoac.com.cn | M2 Science and Technology Museum

YIFU CHINA OPERA THEATRE
逸夫京剧中心 **(134 B3)** *(𝄞 M6)*

Ancient stories of love, death and betrayal; this wonderful masque theatre is a must for lovers of traditional Chinese Kunqu opera. *Fuzhou Lu* 福州路 *701 | tel. 021 63 51 46 68 | M1, M2, M8 People's Square*

WHERE TO STAY

In the luxury, five-star hotels of the metropolis you can float high above the stars – though they are astronomically expensive. But there are also nice starred hostels for people on a modest budget because **World Expo 2010 gave the hotel market a significant boost.**

The needs of business travellers are met by countless mid-range hotels, modern and faceless or bedecked with kitschy adornments. On the other hand, the buildings from the colonial era show a distinctive style and still exude the charm of the 'golden' 1930s. In Mao's time the villas were reserved for the use of politicians and guests of state, and the grand hotels were allowed to become run down, some ending up almost as doss houses. But they have now been luxuriously renovated and are continuing the traditions of the legendary times. In the China of today, small buildings are striving to achieve one special quality, and that is creative charm. Which they're doing successfully! So that even backpackers can now look forward to relaxing in perfectly decent places to stay.

The hotels recommended below are ranked on the basis of the cheapest double room category. The actual price for a night's stay may be considerably higher, for major events for example, but you can also find off-peak special offers which can be significantly cheaper. The usual discounts for internet booking, for example, have been taken into account as well as a frequently charged service fee amounting to 10 to 15% of the room rate.

Photo: Foyer of the Grand Hyatt in the Jin Mao Building

Let your dreams come true: live above the clouds or in splendid colonial hotels – the choice is yours

The most reasonable rates are in general to be obtained by booking early through a travel agent or on the internet, where a wide range of offers can be found in English at *www.elong.net, www.english. ctrip.com* and *www.sinohotel.com*.

Should you turn up at reception without having booked in advance, then you should always have a look at the room before saying you'll take it, and ask for a better one at the same rate should you find anything wrong with it.

The hotels listed below – with the ex-ception of the cheap hostels – all meet a minimum standard, i.e. double rooms with air conditioning, en suite bathroom, TV and telephone, internet/ADSL connec-tion or WIFI in the room or in the busi-ness centre as well as restaurant, services and fitness facilities.

HOTELS: EXPENSIVE

These five star hotels pamper their guests with butler service, sports facili-ties (fitness centre, swimming pool, ten-

Luxury against a fabulous backdrop: the Shangri-La in Pudong

re-emerged in 2009 with the full glory of its Art Deco restored. 96 opulently furnished rooms, many with a small balcony. It's just a very short walk to People's Square and Nanjing Lu. *Hankou Lu* 汉口路 *740 | tel. 021 60 80 08 00 | yangtze boutique.langhamhotels.com | M1, M2, M8 People's Square*

LES SUITES ORIENT 东方商旅酒店 ⚜ (135 D4) (*𝄞 O7*)

Modern elegance is the key characteristic of this 168-room hotel, to which visitors give the very best ratings, ranked number 1 out of 2,694 hotels on one website. Its location on the Bund with a view of Huangpu Yu Garden (best from the 10th floor) is a winning feature, as is its good value for money. *Jinling Donglu* 金陵东路 *1 | tel. 021 63 20 00 88 | www.lessuites orient.com | M10 Yu Garden*

JW MARRIOTT HOTEL AT TOMORROW SQUARE 明天广场JW万豪酒店 ⚜ (134 A2) (*𝄞 L6*)

'Tomorrow Square' is the 60-storey skyscraper on People's Park that looks like a rocket. In some of the 342 rooms you even get a panoramic view of Shanghai from the bath. Expensive, but quite luxurious. Business people love the executive floor. *Nanjing Xilu* 南京西路 *399 | tel. 021 53 59 49 69 | www.marriott.de | M1, M2, M8 People's Square*

PUDONG SHANGRI-LA 浦东香格里拉大酒店 ⚜ (135 E4) (*𝄞 P7*)

Sink back into the deep armchairs in the hotel foyer at teatime, nibble on dainty delicacies and enjoy the view of the Bund listening to live piano music – can life get any lovelier than this! The hotel has more than 606 splendidly decorated rooms and suites in the *River Wing* and 375 super-luxurious rooms in the *Grand Tower*. *Fucheng Lu* 富城路 *33 | tel. 021*

nis, squash), health and beauty salons, fine restaurants, cafés and bars. They also offer a business centre, conference rooms and banqueting and ballrooms.

GRAND HYATT 金茂君悦大酒店 ★ ⚜ (135 F4) (*𝄞 Q7*)

The Jin Mao Building has no equal in terms of elegance. The outstanding hotel satisfies the highest demands: 555 classy suites and luxurious rooms are grouped round a 115-m high atrium. You can also enjoy fine dining in a chic modern atmosphere. *Century Avenue (Shiji Dadao)* 世纪大道 *88 | tel. 021 50 49 12 34 | www. shanghai.grand.hyatt.com | M2 Lujiazui*

LANGHAM YANGTZE BOUTIQUE

朗廷扬子精品酒店 (134 B2) (*𝄞 M6*)
The former Yangtze Hotel was built in 1934 in the Portuguese colonial style and

68 82 88 88 | www.shangri-la.com | M2 Lujiazui

HOTELS: MODERATE

BROADWAY MANSIONS HOTEL
上海大厦 (135 E1) (*⑪ P5*)

An impressive building on the north of the Bund with 253 luxurious and spacious rooms with a classic ambience, and ☀ INSIDER TIP ▸ from the 12th to the 16th floor you can enjoy a panoramic view of the city and the river. *By Suzhou Lu* 北苏州路 *20 | tel. 021 63 24 62 60 | www. broadwaymansions.com*

HENGSHAN MOLLER VILLA 衡山马勒别墅饭店 ★ (133 D2) (*⑪ J6*)

This small, Harry Potter-style castle was built by the Swedish shipping tycoon Eric Möller in 1936. Today the villa offers the latest in comfort and is equipped with chandeliers, brocade curtains and gilded furnishings. The eleven grandiose suites, some with a view of the garden, will please the romantics among you. In the rear courtyard there's a light, friendly new building with 34 rooms. *Shaanxi Nanlu* 陕西南路 *30 | tel. 021 62 47 88 81 | www.mollervilla. com | M1, M10 Shanxi Road South*

JIN JIANG HOTEL 锦江饭店 ☀
(133 D3) (*⑪ K7*)

The Georgian architecture of the former Cathay Mansions, built in the 1920s, is impressive. The tall rooms in the northern Grosvenor House are tastefully furnished with traditional furniture and décor, though they are a little drab, but the southern building has been appropriately modernised. When President Nixon visited China, the American delegation stayed here. It has 442 rooms. *Maoming Nanlu* 茂名南路 *59 | tel. 021 32 18 98 88 | jj.jinjianghotels.com | M1, M10 Shanxi Road South*

OKURA GARDEN HOTEL 花园饭店
(133 D3) (*⑪ J7*)

This elegant Japanese hotel is housed in the 1929 French sports club. In the concrete block to the rear there are 492 brightly furnished rooms. *Maoming Nanlu* 茂名南路 *58 | tel. 021 64 15 11 11 | www.gardenhotelshanghai.com | M1, M10 Shanxi Road South*

PARK HOTEL 国际饭店 ☀
(134 A2) (*⑪ M5–6*)

The Art Deco skyscraper has stood in the geographical centre of the city since 1934. The standard rooms are spacious, but a little dreary. There are 244 rooms, but choose one with a view of People's Park. *Nanjing Xilu* 南京西路 *170 | tel. 021 63 27 52 25 | www.parkhotel.com. cn | M1, M2, M8 People's Square*

PARKVIEW HOTEL 东怡大酒店
(0) (*⑪ 0*)

A beautifully shaped building in Pudong, designed by Paul Andreu, the architect of the adjacent Oriental Art Center, it has 209 comfortable rooms with an appealing design. This is a place to enjoy

★ **Grand Hyatt**
It's been an icon of modern Shanghai since its opening → p. 84

★ **Hengshan Moller Villa**
Stay in a Swedish fairytale castle → p. 85

★ **Fairmont Peace Hotel**
The combination of luxury and location is unique → p. 86

★ **Old House Inn**
Creaky stairs take you up to four-poster beds → p. 89

MARCO POLO HIGHLIGHTS

INSIDER TIP afternoon tea with a view of the green spaces. *Dingxiang Lu* 丁香路 *555 | tel. 021 61 62 11 18 | www.parkview hotel.cn | M2 Science and Technology Museum*

QUINTET (132 B3) (*Ⅲ G7*)

Even if it markets itself as a 'bed & breakfast', this hostel is really a small but very

fine hotel. The six perfectly furnished rooms, distributed over the three floors of the old building, all have individual names. 'Oriental Pearl' for example is on the ground floor and has a veranda and direct access to outside. The hotel is hidden behind the *Closed Door* restaurant. *Changle Lu* 长乐路 *808 | tel. 021 62 49*

LUXURY HOTELS

A bed for the night costs upwards of 2,500 Yuan and suites can be as much as 80,000 Yuan.

Park Hyatt 柏悦酒店 ☆ (135 F4) (*Ⅲ Q7*)

Live up in the sky in the Shanghai World Financial Center, where you'll find all the peace and quiet you need to soothe your frayed nerves. Here luxury means minimalist elegance. Wood and dark stone, bright linen and just a gentle hint of Asia – a refined context for the astonishingly beautiful view from 174 rooms and suites. *Century Avenue* 世纪大道 *100 | tel. 021 68 88 12 34 | shanghai. park.hyatt.com | M2 Lujiazui*

Fairmont Peace Hotel 和平饭店 ★ ☆ (135 D2) (*Ⅲ O6*)

This has been the first port of call on the Bund since 1929 and where the leading figures of society used to live. Later alterations robbed the Art Deco building of much of its charm. But since 2010, after three years of painstaking restoration of all 270 rooms and other spaces, it has been able to enjoy its stylish resurrection – now more luxurious than ever. It's a must for non-residents too, with the bar and jazz band. If you're looking for relaxation, a fragrant

oil massage perhaps, then you'll find it at the outstanding ● *Willow Stream Spa* with pool and glass ceiling. *Nanjing Donglu* 南京东路 *20 | tel. 021 63 21 68 88 | www.fairmont.de | M2, M10 East Nanjing*

Peninsula 半岛酒店 (135 D2) (*Ⅲ P5*)

No one will mind that the Art Deco style is only a modern reconstruction – the 235-room hotel opened in 2010 – and technophiles will love the whole room electronics where everything can be controlled by remote control from the bath! The location on the Bund is sublime and beyond reproach. *Zhongshan Dong Yilu* 中山东一路 *32 | tel. 021 23 27 28 88 | www.peninsula.com*

Ritz-Carlton 浦东丽思卡尔顿酒店 ☆ (135 F3) (*Ⅲ Q7*)

The very name stands for world-renowned luxury. This refined hotel occupies the top 15 floors of the International Finance Centre's south tower and all 285 rooms boast an extensive view. Its outstanding feature is the spa area: 1,500m² with a panoramic view to enjoy as you swim on the 53rd floor. *Century Avenue* 世纪大道 *8 | tel. 021 20 20 18 88 | www.ritzcarlton.com | M2 Lujiazui*

A hint of Spain: architecture with colonial charm in the Anting Villa Hotel

90 88 | www.quintet-shanghai.com | M1, M7 Changshu Road

RADISSON PLAZA XING GUO HOTEL
兴国宾馆 (0) (*M F7*)

An elegant hotel in the heart of the French Concession, and the large, old, peaceful park is very relaxing. The hotel provides 190 rooms, including 40 suites, and also has an excellent swimming pool. *Xingguo Lu* 兴国路 *78 | tel. 021 62 12 99 98 | www. radisson.com/shanghaicn_plaza*

INSIDER TIP ▶ URBN HOTEL 雅悦酒店
(132 B1) (*M H5*)

Here you'll find an artistic combination of the old (bricks, wood and leather cases) with the new (modern, cosmopolitan design). The result is a lovely light hotel, opening onto an old factory's idyllic inner courtyard. And it's not just couples on honeymoon in whom the penthouse will awaken a desire for quiet intimacy for two, and on the terrace you can also celebrate with friends. The 26-room hotel is the first CO_2 neutral hotel in China and there is a clear emphasis here on being environmentally friendly. *Jiaozhou Lu* 胶州路 *183 | tel. 021 51 53 46 00 | www. urbnhotels.com | M2, M7 Jing'an Temple*

HOTELS: BUDGET

INSIDER TIP ▶ ANTING VILLA HOTEL
安亭别墅酒店 (132 A5) (*M G9*)

The hotel with a Spanish flavour has 144 rooms, and you should choose one on the 7th or 8th floor with a view of an old cedar garden. 40 of the rooms are located in a villa, and the suites there are furnished in the Empire style. *Anting Lu* 安亭路 *46 | tel. 021 64 33 11 88 | www.antingvillahotel-shanghai.com | M1 Hengshan Road*

CAPTAIN HOSTEL 船长青年酒店

The chain has three branches, all of which offer rooms at very reasonable rates in attractive locations: two of them round the corner from the Bund, the other in Pudong. The best run (and most expensive) is the one in Yan'an Lu (60 rooms), where a roof garden is a really attractive feature. Among the 30 rooms of the Laoshan Lu branch there are some very reasonably priced single rooms. The main branch in Fuzhou Lu also has 30 rooms. The designation 'hostel' refers to the fact that sleeping is dormitory style (not in Pudong). *Fuzhou Lu* 福州路 *37 | tel. 021*

www.citadines.com/de/index.html | M1 Xinzha Road

CITY HOTEL 城市酒店
(133 D2) *(*🕮 *J6)*
It's grey outside but good inside, well furnished and with good service, rates and view from the ☼ upper floors. There are

Here it's quite cheap to go on board: double cabin in the Captain Hostel

63 23 50 53 | M2, M10 East Nanjing Road **(135 D3)** *(*🕮 *O6); Laoshan Lu* 崂山路 *527 | tel. 021 58 36 59 66 | M2, M4, M6, M9 Century Avenue* **(0)** *(*🕮 *S9); Yan'an Donglu* 延安东路 *7A, tel. 021 33 31 00 00 | M10 Yu Garden* **(135 D3)** *(*🕮 *O7) | www.captainhostel.com.cn*

CITADINES JINQIAO 馨乐庭金桥服务公寓 **(134 A1)** *(*🕮 *M5)*
The centrally located apartment hotel, not far from People's Square, provides 260 living units (studios and multi-room apartments) with kitchen and may well be of particular interest to families with small children. It can also be booked for just one night. There are dishwashers and microwaves in the kitchens. *Beijing Xilu* 北京西路 *55 | tel. 021 23 08 66 66 |*

276 rooms. Shaanxi Nanlu 陕西南路 *5–7 | tel. 021 62 55 11 33 | www.cityhotelshang hai.com | M1, M10 Shanxi Road South*

KOALA GARDEN HOUSE
考拉花园旅舍 **(131 F2)** *(*🕮 *P2)*
Small flowers only bloom here on the wallpaper and curtains, which obscure the view into the rear courtyard, but they also lend the old-fashioned but comfortable hotel a certain endearing charm. Opened in 2009 after a colourful renovation, the small hotel offers 25 reasonably priced rooms, some dormitory style. The friendly staff serve breakfast in the *Eucalyptus Café* with a view of the pedestrian Duolun Lu. *Duolun Lu* 多伦路 *240 | tel. 021 56 71 10 38 | M3, M8 Hongkou Football Stadium*

LING LONG HOTEL 玲珑宾馆
(0) *(₪ E6)*

A B&B in an old Shanghai building with 15 comfortable guest rooms, lovingly furnished in a gently nostalgic style. Breakfast is Chinese and the boss Kathy is the only one of the staff to speak good English. *Yan'an Xilu* 延安西路 *939 | tel. 021 62 25 03 60 | M2, M11 Jiangsu Road*

INSIDER TIP MAGNOLIA 小木兰旅馆
(132 C3) *(₪ H7)*

Bed & Breakfast: Miranda Yao and Norris Chen feel personally responsible for the wellbeing of their guests staying in the five rooms. It has to be said that you pay twice as much as in the Koala Garden or the Ling Long Hotel, but for that you get a genuine nostalgic ambience and a fantastic location in the heart of the old French Concession. *Yanqing Lu* 延庆路 *36 | tel. 021 1 38 17 94 08 48 | www.magnoliabnbshanghai.com | M1, M7 Changshu Road*

MOTEL 168 莫泰 168 **(134 B4)** *(₪ N7)*

Of the various hotel chains in Shanghai, this is the best and you won't find any other hotel in such a central location (near People's Square) for less. But be aware that the cheapest of the 239 rooms are narrow and relatively noisy. *Jinling Donglu* 金陵东路 *531 | tel. 021 51 53 33 33 | M8 Dashijie*

OLD HOUSE INN 老时光酒店 ★
(132 B2) *(₪ G–H7)*

This 1930s' style old English house lies hidden away in an alley. It's very different from the modern hotels and quiet and comfortable. Yellow walls and Chinese furniture decorate the twelve small rooms, which have modern bathrooms. The four-poster bed in room 203 is particularly attractive! *Huashan Lu Lane 351 no. 16* 华山路351弄16号 *| tel. 021 62 48*

61 18 | www.oldhouse.cn | M2, M7 Jing'an Temple

SEAGULL HOTEL 海鸥饭店 ☆
(135 E2) *(₪ P5)*

There are 149 comfortably furnished rooms. Where Suzhou Creek feeds into the Huangpu, you have a fantastic view of the city, so it's worth paying a little extra to upgrade to a river view. *Huangpu Lu* 黄浦路 *60 | tel. 021 63 25 15 00 | www.seagull-hotel.com*

LOW BUDGET

▶ *City Central International Hostel:* Near the Metro and completely refurbished, the hostel is very highly rated by visitors. 150 rooms, beds from 50 Yuan. *Wuning Lu Lane 300 no. 50 | tel. 021 52 90 55 77 | M3, M4, M11 Cao-yang Road | (0) (₪ F2)*

▶ *Mingtown Etour Youth Hostel:* new hostel in the old construction style, the courtyard is a little oasis. Beds from 50, double rooms from 150 Yuan. *Jiangyin Lu 55 | tel. 021 63 27 77 66 | M1, M2, M8 People's Square (133 F2) (₪ L6)*

▶ *Mingtown Hiker Youth Hostel:* lovely accommodation in an old building. Beds from 55 Yuan, double rooms from 170 Yuan. *Jiangxi Zhonglu 450 | tel. 021 63 29 78 89 | M2, M10 Nanjing Road East (135 D1) (₪ O5)*

▶ You can book and find other reasonably priced hostels at *www.hostelworld.com, www.travellerspoint.com w.yhachina.com.*

HANGZHOU & SUZHOU

'Heaven above, Suzhou and Hangzhou below.' If you go to one of these two cities, both steeped in tradition, you'll hear this old aphorism from every Chinese tour guide.

But there's no doubt: as you arrive in these cities from Shanghai, different though they are, you now become truly immersed in the China of old for the first time. They've left their mark on the country's wonderful aesthetic sense for gardens and landscape, and they're the source of silk and tea, two of the exports for which China was renowned centuries or even millennia ago, and which made both cities rich.

Thanks to the high speed trains, one day is just about adequate for a quick visit to each, but only 'just about'. Two days for each would be much better and three wouldn't be overdoing it.

HANGZHOU

杭州

MAP ON PAGE 142

(140 C5) *(∅ 0)* **Hangzhou – The West Lake, shrouded in legend, celebrated in thousands of songs, an inspiration for poets and painters, has been attracting visitors for centuries.**

Even emperors came to delight in the place's beauty. The city enjoyed its greatest flowering as the capital of the Southern Song Dynasty (1127–79). Marco Polo, visiting shortly afterwards, thought it the most beautiful place on earth.

Photo: Zhuozheng Yuan Garden in Suzhou

Heaven on earth: Hangzhou and Suzhou offer the classical Chinese aesthetic sense of landscape, imbued with significance

CITY WHERE TO START?

Hangzhou starts and finishes with the **West Lake (142 B–C 3–4)** (*Ø 0*). No matter where you come down to its shores, you're in just the right place for an extended walk. And the city promenade is the perfect starting place for boat trips (by ferry to the islands or on a hand-steered gondola), though there are also jetties elsewhere.

With four million inhabitants, Hangzhou is now the capital of Zhejiang Province. At the southern end of the Grand Canal of China and 200km (125mi) from Shanghai, it's been part of the rapid development of the lower Yangtze area.

SIGHTSEEING

HEFANG JIE 河坊街 &
WU SHAN 吴山 **(142 C3–4)** (*Ø 0*)
A decorative gate leads into Hefang Jie, a pedestrian replica of an Old Town. A

colourful range of goods and traditional eating places successfully create a delightful ambience. A high wall on the southern side conceals the city's most beautiful historic property: the Hu Qingyu Tang pharmacy founded in 1874 with a INSIDER TIP *Museum of Traditional Chinese Medicine (daily 8.30am–5pm | admission 10 Yuan | www.hqyt.com).* The premises themselves are worth seeing with their planted inner courtyards and gilded carvings.

River and is on an extraordinarily large scale. Its name evokes the six-fold unity of the community of monks. Just under 60m high, the wooden construction dates from 1900, the brick core concealed within dating from 1153. You can also undertake a short educational trip to find out more about pagodas on the wooded slope behind the pagoda, where models of the country's famous pagodas have been built to a scale from 1:5 to 1:10, and there are also explanatory text panels.

One of more than 300 sculptures in the cliff: laughing pot-bellied Buddha on the Feilai Feng

The hill immediately to the south of the gate is called the Wu Shan. It's laid out as a park, topped since 2000 by the ☀,City God Pavilion' *Chenghuang Ge (daily 7.30am–10pm | admission 30 Yuan)*, a huge tower with typical Chinese roof and lift to take you up to the best view of the city and lake. A large diorama shows Hangzhou as it was in the 13th/14th centuries.

LIUHE TA PAGODA 六和塔 ☀
(142 B5–6) (ﻼ 0)
The 'Six Harmonies Pagoda' stands on a small hill with a view over the Qiantang

Daily 6am–6pm | admission 30 Yuan incl. ascent of tower | 3km south of the West Lake above the Qiantang Jiang Bridge

PROVINCIAL MUSEUM 浙江省博物馆
(142 B3) (ﻼ 0)
These classical buildings hold a great variety of beautifully presented exhibits, labelled in English: archaeological finds of prehistoric cultures, ceramics, coins, craftwork, plastics and sculptures, paintings and calligraphy. *Mon midday–4.30pm, Tue–Sun 9am–4.30pm (admission until 4pm) | admission free | Gu Shan Island | Gu-shan Lu 孤山路 25*

SILK MUSEUM 中国丝绸博物馆 (142 B4) (🛱 0)

The front is more a department store, the rear provides information on the history and technology of silk production, and 1,000-year old silks are the outstanding highlight. *Daily 8.30–4.30pm (admission till 4pm) | admission free | Yuhuang Shan Lu* 玉皇山路 *73 | south of the lake*

TEA MUSEUM 中国茶叶博物馆 ● (142 A4) (🛱 0)

This shows the history and culture of tea planting, processing and preparation in a lovely setting. *Tue–Sun 8.30–4.30pm | admission free | Longjing Lu* 龙井路 | *Shuangfeng Cun* 双峰村 *(southwest of the lake)*

LINGYIN SI TEMPLE 灵隐寺 AND FEILAI FENG MOUNTAIN 飞来峰 ★ (142 A3) (🛱 0)

The exotic sounding names 'Temple of the Soul's Retreat' and 'The Flying Peak' conceal but perhaps hint at a remarkable juxtaposition of nature and religious art: there's a shaded valley with a stream and on one side a cliff decorated by ancient sculptures, and on the other an impressive Buddhist temple.

The monastery is said to have been founded by an Indian monk in 326 who thought the rocky hill opposite (170m/560ft high) looked like a mountain from his homeland – as though it had flown miraculously all the way to China. Later, from the 10th–14th centuries, more than 300 Buddhist sculptures and reliefs were hewn out of the rock, most of them in natural grottos. The most famous statue, near the temple, is a laughing pot-bellied Buddha dating from the Song Dynasty.

None of the present monastery buildings is more than 150 years old, and this applies not only to the two stone Sutra columns by the path at the front – which were made in 1969 – but also to the two battered stone pagodas from the same era in the first courtyard. In the middle of the *Hall of the Heavenly Kings* there is the cheerful pot-bellied Buddha; at the back is Weituo, guardian of monasteries and Buddhist teaching, both housed in magnificent shrines; and arranged along the sides stand the four Heavenly Kings, protectors of the earth and fighters against all evil.

The 33-m (108ft) high *Grand Hall* dating from 1953 can be rather overpowering. It houses a 9-m (30-ft) high Shakyamuni Buddha, carved from camphor wood and gilded in 1956; including its base and gloriole, the work of art attains a height of almost 20m (65ft). The figures to the sides are the 20 arhats of Buddhism, and behind them are the Buddha's enlightened pupils. At the back a 20m high relief depicts the history of the novice Shan Cai

---

Chatting at the Lingyin Si Temple

seeking out 53 teachers as he makes his way towards attaining Buddhahood. In the centre stands Guanyin, the Goddess of Mercy, shown standing on the head of an enormous fish, which bears her across the ocean so that she can come to people's salvation.

You then come to the *Hall of the Medicine Buddha* surrounded by his two helpers and the twelve patron saints to the twelve double hours of the day. The final two halls with their statues were not completed until 2000, the last hall but one (with its huge granite relief) housing the monastery's treasury.

The mighty *Hall of the 500 Arhats* just to the west of the *Hall of the Heavenly Kings* has a complex floor plan in the shape of a Buddhist manji (whirlwind). The larger than life statues of the holy monks are the largest of their kind in China, giving you a clear idea how this monastery is thriving today. *Daily 7–5pm | entrance for the valley area 35 Yuan, for the monastery an extra 30 Yuan | buses Y1 and Y2 from the city centre to the terminus*

WEST LAKE 西湖 ★
(142 B–C 3–4) (*Ø 0*)
From a bay in the Qiantang River mouth, some 12,000 years ago a spit created a fresh water lake, now the most famous lake in the whole of China. Banks lined with willows, promenades, teahouses, pagodas, boats large and small, islands, lotus, modest hills – the lake, only about 1.5m deep and measuring approx. 6 sq mi, offers all sorts of scenic landscapes and so many ways to enjoy yourself, the loveliest being a round trip of the lake on the INSIDER TIP hand-steered gondolas for up to six people at a fixed price of about 80 Yuan an hour. Alternatively, you can take out a rowing boat or a motorboat. It's best to take your cruise INSIDER TIP late in the afternoon when it's less busy on the water and the islands. You can do a land-based tour using open electric vehicles, which travel along the lake shore.

Xiao Yingzhou, 'Little Yingzhou', takes its name from an island in the ocean where the immortals are said to live – a sort of island paradise. It consists mainly of large ponds bedecked with lotus and water lily. Three stone lanterns called *Santan Yinyue,* 'Three Pools Mirroring the Moon', shine out from the water on its southern

edge. This is one of the ten famous West Lake sights, but the lighted lanterns can only be observed by moonlight at the mid-autumn festival. *Ferry plus entry to the island 45 Yuan Bai Causeway:* the shorter of the two causeway paths takes you from the town promenade to Gu Shan Island. Its name is connected to the poet Bai Juyi who sang its praises in the 9th century. Looking to the northwest you can see the 45-m (148-ft) high *Baochu Pagoda*.

● *Gu Shan Island:* The only natural island in the West Lake is mostly laid out as a park. On its southern bank there are teahouses and restaurants and in between the Provincial Museum. The view from the terrace at its eastern end is famous, the spot poetically known as 'Autumn Moon over the Calm Lake'. To the west, before the causeway deviates to the right, nestling against the hillside, is the beautiful, classical estate of the Xiling Society of Seal Arts dating from 1904 *(admission free)*. *Sun Yat-sen Park* with its many trees takes up most of the island's surface area beyond the buildings lining the causeway. In the northwest near the bridge taking you back to the mainland, the causeway passes the grave of the revolutionary and women's rights activist Qiu Jin (1875–1907).

● *Su Causeway:* The longer of the two causeways was named after Su Dongpo, the poet and state official who had it built from 1089. The 2.8km/1.7mi long causeway takes you across six bridges. Just before the southern end to the right you'll see the lovely *Huagang Park (daily open 24 hours | admission free)* with a teahouse and lots of views over the water.

There are numerous stories and sagas woven round West Lake, the best-known being the one about the White Snake. It's a love story which ends with the trapped snake – in the form of a beautiful lady – being freed from her prison beneath the *Leifeng* Pagoda when the pagoda collapses – which actually happened in 1924. The tower now stands here again, rather ostentatiously, on a hill by the south bank.

Total relaxation in Hangzhou: a gondola ride with friends across the West Lake

YUE-FEI TEMPLE 岳庙 (142 B3) (*ɸ 0*)
General Yue Fei (1103–41) successfully defended China against foreign invaders, but he also lost his life in a court intrigue, posthumously becoming a national hero. He's honoured here along with his parents, and his son's grave is also to be found here. There are cast iron statues portraying his betrayer, the traitor's wife and his two accomplices, forced to kneel before Yue Fei's tomb, and for generations Chinese have spat down on these statues. *Daily 7am–5.30pm | Admission 25 Yuan | Beishan Lu 北山路 | At the north end of the Su Causeway*

INSIDER TIP **COSTA COFFEE**
(142 C3) (*ɸ 0*)
This is the place to go for a coffee with an authentic ambience. *Nanshan Lu 南山路 147 | Xihu Tiandi 西湖天地, Building 11 | Tel. 0571 87 02 71 68 | Budget*

INSIDER TIP **GREEN TEA** 绿茶餐厅
(142 A4) (*ɸ 0*)
If you fancy good traditional food and a view of tea fields and ponds, then make for this restaurant near the Tea Museum. You can also sit outside, but make sure you don't miss out on the excellent fruit juices! *Longjing Lu 龙井路 83 | tel. 0571 87 88 80 22 | Budget*

LOUWAILOU 楼外楼
(142 B3) (*ɸ 0*)
Founded in 1848, this is the outstanding Hangzhou inn, where you can enjoy the well-known specialities such as West Lake Vinegar Fish in a brown sauce, Dragon Well Tea Shrimp and Beggar's Chicken. Remember to reserve a window seat. *Gu Shan Island | Gushan Lu 孤山路 30 | tel. 0571 87 96 90 23 | Moderate*

WANGHU LOU 望湖楼 ●
(142 B2) (*ɸ 0*)
In the 'Lake View House' you can try the famous Longjing (Dragon Well) tea. *Beishan Lu 北山路 12 | At the north end of the Bai Causeway, corner Baochu Lu | Budget*

The best present to bring back from Hangzhou is the green Longjing (Dragon Well) tea, which is available in lots of places. A small tea service from Yixing-Ton would make a splendid complement.

FRIENDSHIP HOTEL 友好饭店
(142 C3) (*ɸ 0*)
230 rooms, central location near the lake, good service, fabulous revolving restaurant. *Pinghai Lu 平海路 53 | tel. 0571 87 07 78 88 | www.friendship-hotel. com | Budget*

XIZI BINGUAN (WANGZHUANG)
西子宾馆 (汪庄) (142 B4) (*ɸ 0*)
This former state-run guesthouse turns its rather unfavourable location at the south end of the lake to its advantage because here you stay in a park-like property on the lakeshore. 200 rooms distributed over 8 buildings. *Nanshan Lu 南山路 37 | tel. 0571 87 02 18 88 | www. xizihotel.com | Moderate*

IMPRESSION WEST LAKE
印象西湖 ★ (142 B3) (*ɸ 0*)
One part of the West Lake is transformed in the evening into a stage for a spectacular show with fantastic light effects. It's fascinating to watch the performers move on the water, and of course the show also involves the telling of a love

story, with music composed by Kitaro. *Daily 7.45pm, duration 60 minutes | admission from 260 Yuan | Opposite the Yue-Fei Temple | tel. 0571 87 96 22 22*

SUZHOU

苏州

MAP OF PAGE 143

(141 D3) *(ℳ 0)* **China's largest silk-making centre once set the standards for a refined lifestyle, a sense of which can still be gained today from the ★ *Classical Gardens* – and there are more than a dozen for you to visit, the best of them now on Unesco's list of World Heritage Sites.**

Suzhou (pop. 2.4 million) was, after Peking, the second largest city in China until the 19th century. Lots of Confucian officials came from here because the high standard of living generated by the silk industry enabled more families than elsewhere to pay for a good education for at least one son. When these officials

WHERE TO START?
Classical gardens and Suzhou Museum (143 E–F 2–3) *(ℳ 0)*: In Suzhou the practically adjacent Zhuozheng Yuan and Shizilin gardens can be combined with the Suzhou Museum to provide a crash course in all matters to do with horticulture and classical culture.

then settled down to enjoy their retirement, they would tend their gardens as an earthly paradise, far removed from the world of politics.

The city, crisscrossed by many canals, has today become a hi-tech location by virtue of a huge development zone outside the Old Town. The most famous gardens are usually overrun, so do your best to get there as the gates open (admission until half an hour before closing). A *boat trip* round the Old Town takes 80 minutes. Jetty: *Panxu Lu* 盘胥路 *798 | tel. 0512 68 11 80 88* **(143 E3–4)** *(ℳ 0)*

An intricate canal network and hundreds of stone bridges are the defining features of Suzhou

Pavilions are reflected in the goldfish pond: scene in the Liu Yuan Classical Garden

SIGHTSEEING

WUMEN QIAO BRIDGE 吴门桥
(143 E4) (*0*)

The street leading to the bridge is very touristy, but from the highest point of the arched bridge you can view a preserved section of the city wall with a gate, the wide moat and an old pagoda.

CANGLANG TING GARDEN 沧浪亭 ●
(143 E3) (*0*)

This is the oldest of the Suzhou gardens and dates back to the 10th century, gaining its present form in 1873. Its name 'Canglang Pavilion' alludes to an old story telling of a fisherman on the Canglang River who once advised an official to take flight from the falseness of politics and to find happiness in private life. The garden's distinctive feature is the incorporation of a public canal, which enables people passing by in a gondola to be observed through the windows of a double colonnade. In 1927 an art academy was built in the grounds and in 1932 a new building was added next door which is now used as an art gallery. *Daily 8–5pm | admission 16 April–30 Oct 20 Yuan, otherwise 15 Yuan | Cang-lang-ting Jie 沧浪亭街 | entry over the bridge*

LIU YUAN GARDEN 留园
(143 D2) (*0*) ●

With an area of 5 acres, the 'Lingering Garden' is one of the biggest in the city – and is arguably the most varied. Nowhere else is so much play made of the principle of the 'garden within the garden', especially in the eastern half with more

struction been pursued with so much devotion as here, with the paths winding their way through tunnels and grottos. A stone engraving shows what the garden looked like in 1373. Its present form dates from about 1920 – with the addition of elements of a very contrasting style such as the stone ship made of cement. *Daily 7.30am–5.30pm, in winter 8am–5pm | admission 16 April–30 Oct 30 Yuan, otherwise 20 Yuan | Yuan-lin Lu* 园林路 *23*

TINGFENG YUAN GARDEN 听枫园 ●
(143 E2–3) (𝄃 0)

Why not try a visit to one of the less well-known gardens? It'll be far less overrun by tourists. And this one, the 'Listening to Maples Garden', has an area of just 1300 sq m, making it quite intimate. It belongs to the Academy of Traditional Chinese Painting. Extra treat: a teahouse. *Daily 8.30am–8pm | admission free (teahouse: minimum spend 100 Yuan per person) | Qingyuan Fang* 庆元坊 *12 (Branches off Mayike Lu* 马医科路*)*

than a dozen mini scenes, some hardly larger than a room. The more extensive western part makes a conscious attempt to create an impact, with the garden pond, bizarre rocky cliffs and ancient trees. This is where the tour starts. The best way to see all the scenes is to go left round the pond, then over the 'Little Paradise Island', after a few steps along the eastern bank then north again and finally into the eastern part. *Daily 7.30am–5.30pm, in winter 7.30am–5pm | admission 16 April–30 Oct 40 Yuan, otherwise 30 Yuan | Liuyuan Lu* 留园路 *338*

SHIZI LIN GARDEN 狮子林
(143 E–F2) (𝄃 0)

Its name 'Lion Grove' derives from the monastery to which it once belonged. Nowhere else has the art of rockery con-

WANGSHI YUAN GARDEN 网师园
(143 F3) (𝄃 0)

The smallest of the gardens is perfect. Its name 'Garden of the Master of the Nets' takes up the popular topic of the fisherman, because old Chinese fishing tales liked to expand on the utopia of a quiet and peaceful life far removed from politics. This is a particularly good place to gain a good impression of the ideal way to live. From the entrance area go immediately to the left and at first a rocky hill blocks the view of the garden pond, but this only serves to heighten the expectation – and that's as it should be! *Mid Nov–End Feb daily 7.30am–5pm, otherwise 7.30am–5.30pm | admission 16 April–30 Oct 30 Yuan, otherwise 20 Yuan | side street off Daichengqiao Lu* 带城桥路阔家头巷

Fashion show at the monastery: the Taoist Xuanmiao Guan Temple in Suzhou

ZHUOZHENG YUAN GARDEN 拙政园 (143 E–F1) (📖 0)

The 'Humble Administrator's Garden' is the largest of the gardens, its name deriving from a former owner who, at last able to relieve himself of the burden of service to the state, explained: 'As far as my humble self and politics are concerned, it's now a matter of watering trees and planting vegetables'. The garden's best features are the lotus ponds, the distant view of the North Temple pagoda and the associated Bonsai cultivation (at the park's western edge). In the eastern part you can enjoy a rest in the teahouse. *Daily 7.30am–5.30pm, in winter 8am–5pm | admission 16 April–30 Oct 70 Yuan, otherwise 50 Yuan | Dongbei Jie 东北街 178*

NORTH TEMPLE AND PAGODA 北寺塔 ⚓ (143 E1–2) (📖 0)

It's well worth going to the top of the 76-m (250-ft) high Beisi Ta pagoda, the Old Town's highest tower, for the wonderful view. To the east of the pagoda stands the 400-year old Guanyin Hall, the best Ming dynasty building in the city. The temple garden is an oasis of peace and quiet. *Daily 8am–6pm | admission 15 Yuan | Renmin Lu 人民路 652*

SILK MUSEUM 丝绸博物馆 (143 E1–2) (📖 0)

The modern building illustrates the technology and history of silk production. *Daily 9am–5pm | admission free | Renmin Lu 人民路 661 | opposite the Beisi Ta pagoda*

SUZHOU MUSEUM 苏州博物馆 ● (143 E–F1) (📖 0)

This new building, opened in 2006 with a modern garden, was designed by leading architect Ieoh Ming Pei for the city of his forefathers. The exhibits display local art and culture. The attached Residence with an old auditorium was occupied in 1863 by the leaders of the Taiping Rebellion. *Tue–Sun 9am–5pm (admission until 4pm) | admission free | Dongbei Jie 东北街 204*

XUANMIAO GUAN TEMPLE 玄妙观
(143 E2) (*ΩΩ 0*)

The Taoist sanctuary by the popular pedestrian zone marks the centre of the city with its mighty main hall. To the left and right of the square in front stand some smaller temples (same admission ticket), in the entry hall six generals stand guard. The Three Pure Ones, the high deities in the Taoist pantheon, sit on their thrones in the main hall; behind you can see statues of the gods of the 60-year cycle. *Daily 7.30am–4.45pm | admission 10 Yuan | in the middle of Guanqian Jie* 观前街

CALIFORNIA DREAM 加州风情
(143 E2) (*ΩΩ 0*)

Cheese cake, toast, tiramisu, mango mousse, coffee... go to the upper floor! *Furenfang Xiang 22 | To south of the Xuanmiao Guan | Budget*

SONGHELOU 松鹤楼 (143 D2) (*ΩΩ 0*)

The classic Suzhou restaurant – first mentioned in documents in 1757, though this branch is utterly modern, even outdoing its main outlet with its excellent cuisine with dishes typical of the local area. Very decent prices. *Jasmine Holiday Inn, 5th floor| Changxu Lu* 阊胥路 *345 | tel. 0512 65 58 35 83 | Moderate*

WHERE TO STAY

INSIDER TIP ▶ GARDEN VIEW HOTEL 人家大酒店 (143 E–F2) (*ΩΩ 0*)

189 rooms with traditional Chinese ambience! And the centrally located pedestrian zone is just a few minutes' walk away, as is the 'Humble Administrator's Garden'. *Lindun Lu, Luogua Qiao 66* 临顿路落瓜桥下塘 *| tel. 0512 67 77 88 88 | Budget*

PAN PACIFIC 泛太平洋酒店
(143 E4) (*ΩΩ 0*)

484 luxury rooms in the Old Town district, direct access to Panmen Park with pagoda and city wall. *Xinshi Lu* 新市路 *259 | tel. 0512 65 10 33 88 | www.panpacific. com | Moderate*

INSIDER TIP ▶ CULTURAL PROGRAMME IN WANGSHI YUAN GARDEN 网师园 夜花园 (143 F3) (*ΩΩ 0*)

Classic culture in a first-class ambience: in the course of two hours you wander in groups from one station to the next. Music, operatic arias, dance and burlesque – a happy combination even though it's not easy to enjoy in a totally relaxed way because of the large numbers of visitors. *March–Nov daily 7.30pm | tickets (80 Yuan) obtainable at the entrance*

LOW BUDGET

▶ *Hefang Jie street in Hangzhou:* On Hefang Jie and the streets (142 C3) (*ΩΩ 0*) to the north, you can eat both very reasonably and in an authentic setting.

▶ The *West Lake Youth Hostel* in Hangzhou, situated next to the lake, offers beds from 40 Yuan. *Nanshan Lu 62–63 | tel. 0571 87 02 70 27 | www. westlakehostel.com* (142 B4) (*ΩΩ 0*)

▶ In the *Minghantang Youth Hostel* in Suzhou, rich in Old Town ambience, beds for the night start from 20 Yuan. *Guangji Lu Xiatang 61 | tel. 0512 65 83 33 31 | www.mhthostel. com* (143 D2)

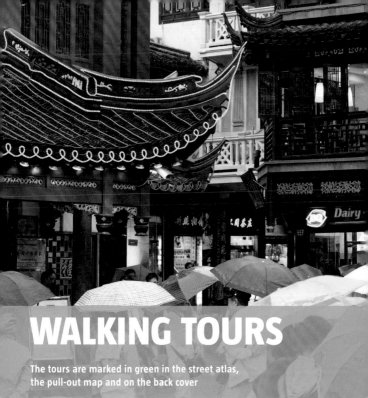

WALKING TOURS

The tours are marked in green in the street atlas, the pull-out map and on the back cover

1 THE AUTHENTIC CHINA

The exuberant, concentrated vitality in the old heart of the city is addictive. Stroll around, look on in amazement and do some shopping: and you should allocate at least five hours to fit all of this in.

This walk begins at the Old City gate, at the corner of Renmin and Lishui Lu. Opposite you'll see the Yuyuan Bazaar → p. 73 complex which is a new building in the style of the Qing dynasty and serves as a temple to consumerism. The shops to the left in Fuyou Lu sell the typical red and gold decorations. Shop no. 11C offers brushes made of natural hair, paper and accessories for calligraphy. On the right,

behind the high wall, you can see the sweeping roofs of the Yu Yuan → p.35. Bear right into Anren Lu and go through the alley along the park wall. Here you'll see people cooking in dark rooms, eating at shop counters, repairing shoes or sewing trousers in small workshops, hawking small items in house doorways and airing mattresses on the pavement; washing is hung out to dry on poles sticking out of the windows. Go twice right and you'll come to the City God Temple (Cheng-huang Miao) → p. 34. The small square in front is filled with the shouts of market traders and the voices of the many people who come to the countless shops. Aromas to whet your appetite emanate from pubs and hot food stalls and mix with the smoke from the large

Photo: Yuyuan Bazaar

A stroll through the centuries – from the Old City to the futuristic Pudong – is a sensuous delight

fire where the faithful light their incense sticks. The shop on the left selling devotional objects beckons with its marvellous kitsch and the sounds of Buddhist cassette recordings. Bu contrast, Yu Yuan Garden is an oasis of ancient Chinese aesthetics and also a haven of peace and quiet, if it's not momentarily overrun by groups of tourists. After the obligatory photo at the Zigzag Bridge make your way through the crowds to Jiujiaochang Lu in the west from which Chenxiangge Lu branches off. Well hidden in the little

alley at no. 29 you'll find a 400-year-old convent *(daily 7am–4pm | admission 10 yuan)*. Now retrace your steps to Old China Street (Fangbang Lu): the four-storey building at the corner of Henan Lu is where countless junk dealers peddle their wares.

Go north on Henan Lu and then turn left into Dajing Lu. Stroll through the lively market street and past remarkably old two-storey buildings. The whole Old City district is threatened by destruction and one glance into the damp, cheerless and dilapidated houses all tightly squeezed together is enough to show that the fabric of the buildings is beyond repair. The occupants are being relocated to satellite towns on the outskirts of the city, as only very few of them can afford somewhere to live in the luxurious apartment blocks which are already shooting up all around. Finally, pay a visit to the Taoist White Cloud Temple (Baiyun Guan | daily 8am–4.30pm | admission 5 yuan) which had to be relocated at Dajing Lu 239 to make way for a high-rise building. Next door you can view the remains of the city wall from the Dajing Tower (daily 9am–4pm | admission 5 yuan).

2 FRENCH FLAIR

A four-hour stroll through the former French Concession where the atmosphere of a past age mixes with the busy Chinese present. Start at a place of entertainment, at the Changle Lu/Maoming Nanlu crossroads where the city's first European theatre is located. In today's Lanxin Theatre, built in 1931 in the style of the Italian Renaissance, ensembles from all over the world give guest performances. The striking 1929 Jin Jiang Hotel → p. 85 is reminiscent of the Georgian period in England and is set off by two gardens. The exclusive Cercle Sportif Français used to be situated opposite and it was the only club, so typical of the French, to accept women as members and later the first to accept Chinese too. The neoclassical building is one of the best loved works by the architect Paul Veysseyre. The interior fittings were glamorous. Mao Zedong, the peasant's son who had survived the hard war years and experienced so much deprivation, picked out the club as a private residence for himself and his followers and eradicated the western luxury, but the old glamour has been brought back in the restoration by the Okura Garden Hotel → p. 85. You can admire the golden wall mosaic in the eastern entrance hall, the staircase with the railings imported from

Savoir-vivre away from the main streets: café district in the French Concession

France as well as the splendid 1930s ball room with its coloured glass roof. And there's also a rooftop terrace and coffee shop.

Cross Huaihai Lu and go along Maoming Lu. The Astrid Apartments, the building to the left on the corner of Nanchang Lu, was built in 1933 in the Art Deco style. If you climb to the sixth floor you can enjoy a splendid view of both the Astrid Apartments and Grosvenor House. Then go right into Nanchang Lu and through the gate on the left hand side of the street into Lane No. 201 and you're now in the heart of the French Concession! Stroll through the quiet, tree lined rear courtyards, past the King Albert Apartments built in the 1930s and come out into Shaanxi Nanlu (no. 157). Follow the street and then turn right into the small alley 550 and go past the fruit and vegetable market and take a break in one of the pubs in the Jiashan Market → p. 59. Go back to Shaoxing Lu where Chinese city life shows its leisurely side, turn left at the Ruijin Lu junction with Fuxing Lu, go right and then left into Sinan Lu. This district is characterised by living accommodation from the colonial times, and there are gardens which have been allowed to grow wild where you'll find little jewels, neglected but nonetheless still lovely. The Sun Yat-sen Residence → p. 41 shows how cultured Chinese citizens lived once upon a time. Turn left into Gaolan Lu and have a look inside the Russian Orthodox St Nicholas Church. The once French Fuxing Park → p.39 is typically Chinese, which has something to do with the old men who meet here to chat and play cards. Many of them now have to accept a longer journey to get here because they have been relocated as part of the urban redevelopment programme and now live in anonymous satellite towns. Finally, at the Nanchang

Lu park exit, go across Chongqing Nanlu and follow Xingye Lu till you get to the trendy Xintiandi district where you'll be impressed by the astonishing range of lovely shops.

3 COLONIAL TIMES MEET THE MODERN ERA

An excursion in the city's colonial past through the former International Settlement to the Bund and across to modern Pudong. The walk with architectural highlights is a whole day programme.

Where Suzhou Creek joins the Huangpu River, the steel Garden Bridge (Waibaidu Bridge) built in 1906 takes you across the river. This is where, from 1937 to 1945, the border posts marking the Japanese occupied zone to the north of Suzhou Creek stood. Chinese wanting to cross the bridge had to bow to the Japanese guards and wait for a sign to proceed. If they failed to observe the ritual, they were beaten – a humiliation which older people still bitterly remember. From the bridge you have a good view of the Russian Consulate, built in 1917 by the German architect Hans Emil Lieb in the Historicism style. Directly opposite is the Astor House Hotel, a neo-Renaissance building dating from 1860. If the weather's nice, take a break on the terrace of the Seagull Sightseeing Restaurant → p. 64 for a wonderful view of the river and city. On the left you go past the Broadway Mansions → p 33, a 19-floor Art Deco hotel. The district by Suzhou Creek is being redeveloped with the slogan 'Live by the Water'. Follow the new River Promenade as far as Sichuan Lu where you'll find the splendid neoclassical Post Office, a building dating from 1924 with huge columns, the clock tower which can be seen from far and wide and a lovely a roof garden with far-ranging views. It houses a Post Museum *(Wed, Thu, Sat, Sun 9am–4pm | admission 10 yuan)* which is worth a visit. If you cross the bridge on Suzhou Creek, follow the busy shopping street as far as Hongkong Road (Xianggang Lu) and keep left there, you then come to the building of the Christian Literature Society *(Huqiu Lu 128)*, designed in 1930 by the architect

Society. Completed in 1932 based on a design by Palmer & Turner, this master-piece combines Art Deco with Chinese elements, and note the stone lion ornaments on the roof ridge! It has been beautifully restored by British architect David Chipperfield.

In Beijing Lu, with the Oriental Pearl Tower → p. 49 in front of you, head in

Only heaven is higher: on the Oriental Pearl Tower's viewing deck

Ladislaus Hudec, and the vertical design of the facade, with a huge stone arch standing out prominently in the centre, is an example of modern Art Deco.

You now turn to your right: on the right you'll see some of the few remaining shikumen or stone gate houses. This form of construction, so typical of Shanghai, arose with the increasing density of population in the late 19th and early 20th centuries and was much influenced by western architecture. A decorative gable adorns the stone gate through which you step from the street into a narrow dead end alley formed by rows of terraced houses. The very limited space exudes a sense of comfort and safety, but with the growing number of occupants it also led to overcrowding.

You should then pay a visit to no. 20, the Rockbund Art Museum → p. 32 in the building of the former Royal Asiatic

the direction of the Bund. It's worth a short detour into Yuanmingyuan Lu because here you can visit the Rockbund, named after the Rockefeller Foundation which has been redeveloping the neglected district at enormous financial cost. On the left side of the street there's a marvellous collection of buildings to admire, including the China Baptist Publishing Building (no. 209), a Hudec building dating from 1933. On the right beyond the new Peninsula Hotel you'll find the oldest buildings on the Bund: the former British Consulate dating from 1873, which has now been fully restored and converted to use as a state guest house, and the Union Church from 1886. Now walk along the Bund and take time to have a good look at the foyer of the former Hong Kong and Shanghai Bank → p. 30 the inside of which reveals a most impressive splendour. The portal is guarded by two bronze lions, whose claws and noses shine, because rubbing them is said to bring good fortune. During the Cultural Revolution the animals were removed to put an end to the superstitious practice but today, under the new capitalist rules of play, you can once again wish for all the good luck you need. Then walk upstream where the modern skyline of Pudong makes for a fabulous backdrop beyond the ships on the Huangpu. Diagonally opposite the weather signal station dating from 1907 you'll find the jetties for the ferries to Pudong. Take a ferry across the river *(entrance below | price 2 yuan | direction Dongfang Mingzhu Lu)*.

On the the other side of the river the high-rise buildings, the huge scale and the wide streets are reminiscent of America. Keep left and where the Paulaner Brewery is you get access to the River Promenade. It's much quieter here than on the other bank, where masses of people congregate at weekends, and there are lots of food outlets which invite you to take a break and enjoy the view. On Saturdays and Sundays, taking INSIDER TIP high tea in the hall of the very elegant Pudong Shangri-La → p.84 hotel comes with a very strong recommendation, and you can also enjoy live piano music and a spectacular view of the Bund. You then go round the biggest shopping centre in China, the Super Brand Mall → p.69, and keep to the right until you see the Jin Mao Building → p. 49 and the Shanghai World Financial Center → p. 50 towering up in front of you. You can start the evening with dinner in one of the restaurants in the skyscrapers – with a view of the city's sea of lights at night. And after a drink in the Jade Bar on 36 → p. 78 you'll feel as though you're in seventh heaven.

The shortest and most popular connection to the other Huangpu riverbank is via the Bund Sightseeing Tunnel *(daily 8am–10pm | 45 Yuan | entrance at the TV Tower)*: if you like your entertainment a bit louder and more colourful, you can speed beneath the great river in an underground train surrounded by catchy light and sound effects.

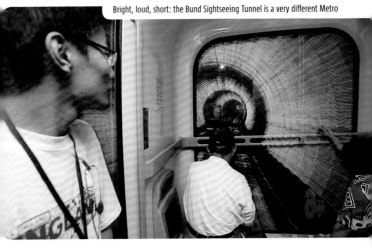

Bright, loud, short: the Bund Sightseeing Tunnel is a very different Metro

TRAVEL WITH KIDS

The Chinese love children. With a little 'treasure' holding your hand, everyone's heart and every camera lens opens. However, it's not possible to guarantee child safety when travelling by taxi, and play equipment in amusement parks does not conform to the standards expected in the UK and USA. Shanghai is therefore not the ideal place for children who are still at the crawling stage, but the city has lots to offer teenagers and children of school age. Let the amazement begin in the Transrapid (free trip for children up to 1.20m/4ft in height) and then, having experienced something futuristic, a more sedate pleasure is perhaps a good idea, like finding your sea legs on a boat trip on the Huangpu River (see 'Travel Tips' chapter).

DINO BEACH WATER PARK
热带风暴水上乐园 (0) (🗺 0)
This water park, with lots of slides, wave pool and paddling areas, can be recommended for little ones on weekdays in the summer. Here it's all about fun, gloriously wet and perhaps a little wild. *Variable opening hours and admission prices| Xinzhen Lu* 新镇路 *78 | www.64783333.com*

GONG THEATRE 共舞台 (134 B3) (🗺 M7)
Kaleido: Eyes of Shanghai is a multi-media road sweeper. His journey through time is presented with a dazzling array of colours, with elements of acrobatics, Asian martial arts, song and dance. *Daily 7.30pm | admission 80–580 yuan | Yan'an Donglu* 延安东路 *433 (Near Xizang Nanlu) | tel. 021 51 09 99 10 | www.era-shanghai.com | M8 Dashijie*

NIHONG KIDS PLAZA 霓虹儿童广场 (134 A3) (🗺 M7)
This paradise is below street level: teddy bears and battery-operated tanks, the whole gamut of the Chinese toy industry, and in addition blouses with little bows and train driver T-shirts: you can buy everything a child yearns for in the underground market. *Pu'an Lu 10* 普安路 *| entrance to south of Yan'an Lu*

AMUSEMENT PARKS
Off to the park if you want to have some fun and let off steam! You'll find play areas in *Lu-Xun Park* (131 F1) (🗺 *P–Q1*) and *Fuxing Park* (133 E4) (🗺 *K8*). Children's entertainments are offered for a few yuan, such as roundabout rides. In the extensive *Century Park (daily 7am–6pm | admission 10 yuan | Jinxiu Lu 1001 | M2*

Transrapid and acrobats: in Shanghai there are a thousand exciting things to discover — and to let off steam there's always the park

Century Park) (0) *(🚇 0)* there's a large lake where you can go on a boat trip and several play areas (separate admission) with a Wild West fort, and you can hire tandems and pedal-driven family cycling cars. And it's an ideal place to fly a kite!

SHANGHAI HISTORY MUSEUM
上海市历史博物馆 **(135 F3)** *(🚇 Q6)*
The city's history is graphically portrayed in the base of the TV Tower, showing you craftsmen's and tradesmen's rooms, places of pleasure and hardship, scenes from the past, and Shanghai's former residents are reproduced almost life-size in the museum which is really worth a visit. Son et lumière effects make it come alive. *Daily 8am–10pm | admission 35 yuan | Gate 4, Century Avenue (Shiji Dadao)* 世纪大道 1 *| www.historymuseum.sh.cn | M2 Lujiazui*

SHANGHAI OCEAN AQUARIUM
上海海洋水族馆 **(135 E3)** *(🚇 0)*
Fish from all over the world are brought together here in the biggest aquarium in Asia. The dangerous sharks and the eerie residents of the deep sea are very impressive. After your visit you can hire a boat in Century Park and look out for a shadow in the water beneath you, which will keep the children in a good mood. *Daily 9am–6pm, in holidays till 9pm (last admission 30 minutes before) | admission 135 Yuan, children 1–1.40m/3ft3in–4ft6in 90 yuan | Lujiazui Ring Road* 陆家嘴环路 *1388 | M2 Lujiazui | www.sh-soa.com/en*

WHEN YOU GET HUNGRY
Children are always very welcome in Shanghai's restaurants. Whilst the children play in the garden, you can have a relaxed Sunday lunch from 1pm at *O'Malleys Irish Pub (p. 79)*. You can enjoy a nice sit by the river in *Originality Street (Jinyan Lu | Cross the wooden bridge south of the Science & Technology Museum)* (0) *(🚇 0)*, where there's a whole row of coffee and teahouses and international restaurant chains such as Starbucks, from where you can enjoy a nice view.

FESTIVALS & EVENTS

There are colourful festivals throughout the year in Shanghai: The Father Christmases continue to twinkle till the Spring Festival, and in autumn and winter the city organises numerous festivals and cultural events.

NATIONAL BANK HOLIDAY

1 Jan New Year; **Spring Festival:** Chinese New Year incl. day before and day after; **Qingming Festival:** a day of mourning for the dead, in leap years and the following year on 4, otherwise 5 April; **1 May** Labour Day; **Dragon Boat Festival** and **Mid-Autumn Festival:** see 'Traditional Festivals'; **1 Oct** National Day (plus two days following)

TRADITIONAL FESTIVALS

The Chinese lunar calendar determines the dates which therefore vary each year.

SPRING FESTIVAL (CHUNJIE)

The city is festooned in decorations for the Chinese New Year Festival. Dragon dances are performed, lots of shops and restaurants are closed. Families celebrate together and the evil spirits of the old year are cast out with fireworks and firecrackers. (10 Feb 2013, 31 Jan 2014) The din and revelry come to an end on the 15th day with the ▶ *Lantern Festival:* brightly coloured lanterns are hung up in the parks and the Yuyuan Bazaar.

DRAGON BOAT FESTIVAL (DUANWUJIE)

Chinese dragons are masters of the water and so this festival was originally a ritual to guard against flooding. Today the celebration is held on the 5th day of the 5th lunar month in honour of the official and poet Qu Yuan (332–296 BC) who drowned himself out of despair at the political state of affairs. During the festival, people delight in eating *zongzi,* rice dumplings wrapped in bamboo leaves. (23 June 2012, 12 June 2013)

MID-AUTUMN FESTIVAL (ZHONGQIUJIE)

In China there's a saying, ‚Marriages are made in heaven and arranged on the moon.' The old man in the moon is called Yue Lao and keeps the large book in which the names of future married couples are noted down. The moon shines particularly brightly on the 15th day of the 8th month. Families come together and eat circular ‚moon cakes' and look at the moon. (30 Sept 2012, 19 Sept 2013)

Whether it's old or new customs, in Shanghai they know how to party whenever there's a reason for dressing up and eating and drinking

FESTIVALS & SPORT

APRIL
▶ *Formula 1:* excitement at the motor racing at the *Shanghai International Circuit* in Anting (Jiading District). *www.formula1.com*

MAY
▶ *Spring International Music Festival:* traditional Chinese and international classical concerts with world-famous musicians

JUNE
▶ *Shanghai International Film Festival:* with exhibitions, retrospectives and appearances of international stars and directors. *www.siff.com*

SEPTEMBER/OCTOBER
▶ *International Music Fireworks Festival:* pyrotechnicians from all over the world display their explosive art to the accompaniment of music and laser effects

SEPTEMBER–NOVEMBER
▶ *International Arts Festival (www.artsbird.com):* music, dance, theatre, art and culture weeks with the ▶ ★ *Shanghai Biennale* (every two years, the next: 2012, 2014; *www.shanghaibiennale.com*) as an international platform for Chinese artists

OCTOBER
▶ *Tourism Festival:* ethnic processions in the gloriously illuminated city. With the *Fengxian Kite Festival* in the Kite Flying Yard in the Fengxian Bay Tourist Zone in the south of the city
▶ *ATP Tennis Masters Cup* in the *Qizhong Stadium (5500 Yuanjiang Lu, Minhang District). www.shanghairolexmasters.com*

NOVEMBER/DECEMBER
▶ *Shanghai Marathon:* last weekend in November or first in December *www.shmarathon.com*

LINKS, BLOGS, APPS & MORE

▶ www.shanghai.gov.cn Shanghai city government's home page. In the top left corner there's a link to the English version. From there you can click on ‹Travel› and you'll find a well organised and well maintained site with lots of up-to-date information on news, what's on, tourist attractions, shopping, bars and restaurants, local travel and maps and lots more

▶ www. smartshanghai.com The site contains a wealth of information and recommendations (with reviews) on shopping, dining, events and nightlife, and there's a very clear Metro map and city street plan

▶ www.urbanatomy.com This is the official home page of the city magazine ‹That's›. Not everything is really relevant (quite a lot is essentially gossip), but if you look under ‹Bars & Clubs›, ‹Arts & Culture› and ‹Events› you'll find lots of topical information

▶ www.shanghaidaily.com This is the online version of the 'Shanghai Daily' newspaper with lots of tourist information and lots of downloads and apps

▶ http://wikitravel.org/en/Shanghai This provides, as you would expect, a huge amount of very factual information about the city's history, geography and culture, but there are also plenty of tourist tips

▶ http://56minus1.com/ Adam J Schokora, a media specialist from Detroit now living in Shanghai, posts images of quirky urban scenes with a focus on technology, design and social media on his Shanghai blog

▶ phatsh.com/?tag=shanghai A must for foodies! It's all about food. The restaurant addresses are also given in Chinese – utterly delightful

▶ shanghaiist.com First created as a blog, it's now become a professionally run mass event with lots of contributors and more than 200,000 readers a month with links to Facebook and Twitter

Regardless of whether you are still preparing your trip or already in Shanghai: these addresses will provide you with more information, videos and networks to make your holiday even more enjoyable

▶ www.onedir.com Features a collection of several webcams along the Bund and there are also a few Shanghai videos

▶ www.tripfilms.com/Tourism-l62612-Shanghai-Travel_Videos.html A large number of English travel and city videos on Shanghai and other related topics, and some are really witty

▶ http://video.travelchinaguide.com/shanghai/ There are 22 videos of Shanghai, some very short, on a variety of sights and topics

▶ Explore Shanghai The personal companion for Metro trips through the metropolis. For the area surrounding each station Smartphone users can also display the relevant section on Google Maps. English speaking

▶ Catch Your Bus Shanghai The appropriate, English language add-on for what is otherwise a pretty impenetrable bus network, available for iPhones

▶ Shanghai Metro Map Small free app for Android phones – does what is says on the tin. There's a corresponding version for Windows phones: *Shanghai Metro for WP7*

▶ Shanghai WOW! City Guide English city guide for Smartphones, free

▶ forum.virtualtourist.com Much used platform, meaning that you can normally get a pretty quick reply to your question

▶ http://www.shanghaiexpat.com/phpbbforum/ Mainly intended for people staying in Shanghai longer term, but there are sections on travel, food, sport and 'best of'

▶ twitter.com/#!/ThatsShanghai The Twitter feed of the city magazine 'That's' gives information, updated every day, on excursion tips, sports events and lucky draws for free tickets. There are also links to podcasts and all sorts of curiosities

▶ http://twitter.com/#!/shanghaidaily This is mainly a news forum but there are items of interest for tourists staying for just a short time, and there are some lovely pictures

TRAVEL TIPS

ARRIVAL

✈ There are direct flights with Virgin Atlantic, British Airways and China Eastern from London. The flight takes approx. twelve hours. Flights are available from approx. 500 GBP/800 US$. American Airlines, United and China Eastern fly nonstop in about 13 hours to Shanghai from Los Angeles.

All international flights land at Pudong Airport (PVG) some 40km (25mi) east of the city centre. You can get information on the airport and connections to the city at *www.shanghaiairport.com* (or ask for the *Traffic Guide* leaflet at the service counter). You can get into the city: by metro line M2; by taxi *(approx. 200 yuan | Make sure the driver switches on the meter!)* – follow the signs to the taxi rank and don't take a trolley with you!; by airport shuttle bus *(2–30 yuan | daily 6am–11pm | departure at the terminal exits to the metro stations and hotels)*; or

by Maglev (Transrapid) which takes eight minutes to the M2 Longyang Road metro station *(single journey 50 Yuan, with flight ticket on the same day 40 yuan | daily 6.45am–9.42pm | 431kmh/265mph maximum speed only from 6.45am till 5.51pm)*.

Most domestic Chinese flights depart from Hongqiao Airport (SHA) in the west of the city. The new terminal 2 has a connection to the metro lines M2 and M10 and to the high speed train station. Only take taxis from the taxi rank. Buses to Pudong or to the city depart from outside the exit.

🚆 If you arrive at the main railway station **(130 A3)** *(𝄞 L2)*, follow the signs to the taxi rank below the square outside. The entrances to the metro M1 are to the left of the south exit, the north exit takes you to the metro lines M3 and M4. The South Station has connections to the metro lines M1 and M3 and taxi ranks are signposted. High speed trains from Nanjing and Beijing arrive at the new station at Hongqiao Airport where extension works are being carried out until 2030.

RESPONSIBLE TRAVEL

It doesn't take a lot to be environmentally friendly whilst travelling. Don't just think about your carbon footprint whilst flying to and from your holiday destination but also about how you can protect nature and culture abroad. As a tourist it is especially important to respect nature, look out for local products, cycle instead of driving, save water and much more. If you would like to find out more about eco-tourism please visit: *www.ecotourism.org*

BANKS & MONEY CHANGING

Most cash machines accept the main credit/debit cards (Visa, MasterCard, etc). Depending on the card and bank, the withdrawal amount is limited to 1,500 to 3,000 yuan per day. At Pudong Airport you can get cash immediately after passing through passport control at the machines in the luggage hall. You can pay by credit card in all the major hotels and department stores and in some restaurants. You can change cash and

From arrival to weather

Holiday from start to finish: useful addresses and information for your trip to Shanghai

travellers cheques in all banks (standard exchange rate, but to change back you must have your passport and receipt). Banks have varying opening hours (basic hours 9am–4.30pm).

CLIMATE, WHEN TO GO

The best times to travel are spring (March–May) and autumn (Oct–Nov). Minimum and maximum temperatures over the year range from -5°C/23°F in winter to over 40°C/104°F in summer. In the winter it can seem to be even colder because of the high humidity. Even in spring it can be quite unpleasant because of the raw winds blowing in off the sea; in March and April you need to pack a warm pullover and a thick jacket. In the summer it's often unbearably hot and sticky but you also always need a light jacket because of the icy cold of the air conditioning.

CONSULATES & EMBASSIES

UK CONSULATE (132 A4) (*ɰ F–G8*)
Suite 301, Shanghai Centre | 1376 Nan Jing Xi Lu | Shanghai 200040 | tel. 021 32 79 20 00 | http://ukinchina.fco.gov.uk/en/

US CONSULATE (132 B4) (*ɰ G8*)
Westgate Mall, 1038 West Nanjing Road, 8th floor | tel. 021 32 17 46 50 | http://shanghai.usembassy-china.org.cn/

CUSTOMS

You may bring in free of customs duty 400 cigarettes, two bottles of spirits (each 750ml) and currency to the value

BUDGETING

Coffee	from 1.50 GBP/2.30 US$ *for a cup in a café*
Beer	from 1.60 GBP/2.50 US$ *for a glass in a pub*
Soup	0.80–1.60 GBP/1.25–2.50 US$ *for a noodle soup in a small pub*
Silk	from 20–26 GBP/ 32–42 US$ *per metre at the fabric market*
Taxi	6.50–20 GBP/10–32 US$ *for a city centre trip*
Umbrella	6.50–13 GBP/10–20 US$ *for a brolly from a street vendor*

of up to 3,000 GBP/5,000 US$ as well as up to 6,000 Yuan. These amounts may also be taken out again when you leave. Objects of cultural inheritance (antiques) must bear the red seal to be free for export.

Duty-free quantities for entry into the UK: e.g. 200 cigarettes or 50 cigars or 250g tobacco, 1 litre of spirits or strong liqueurs over 22% volume or 2 litres of fortified wine, sparkling wine or other liqueurs that are less than 22% volume, 16 litres of beer and up to £390 worth of all other goods including gifts, perfume and souvenirs.

ELECTRICITY

220V at 50Hz. Most modern hotels have multiple outlets that accept several types of plug but make sure your device is 220V. *See http://electricaloutlet.org/*

EMERGENCY

Ambulance tel. 120 (Chinese)
Fire tel. 119 (Chinese)
Police tel. 110 (ask for 'English Operator')

HEALTH

Mains water is not drinking water but you can use it for brushing your teeth. Immunisations are not compulsory, but protection against tetanus, polio, diphtheria, typhus and hepatitis is recommended. You're also recommended to take out travel and health insurance to cover costs of possible repatriation. Be aware that medical treatment has to be paid for up front and clinics do not accept credit cards.

Hospital with 24-hour accident and emergency: *Hua Shan Hospital | Hua-shan Worldwide Medical Centre | Wulumuqi Zhonglu 12 | tel. 021 62 48 99 99-25 31 | www.sh-hwmc.com.cn* (132 A3) *(ᗰ G7)*; foreign department in Bldg. 1, 8/F (daily 8am–10pm); night-time emergences are treated in the Blue Building (no. 6, 15/F). *Doctor/dentist: Parkway Health Medical Centres | Nanjing Xilu 1376 (in the Shanghai Centre) | tel. 021 64 45 59 99 | www.parkwayhealth.cn* (132 C1) *(ᗰ J5)* where there's also a pharmacy *(No. 206 | daily 9am–9pm)* with English-speaking staff and western medicines.

IMMIGRATION

For entry into China you need a valid passport valid for at least six months and a visa (information and applications at *http://www.visaforchina.org*). Applications must be handed in and collected in person or by a representative at one of China's diplomatic missions. Processing usually takes four working days. Places issuing visas are:

UK
– *Embassy of the People's Republic of China | Consular dept.: 31 Portland Place | London W1B 1JL | tel. 020 76 31 14 30 | http://www.chinese-embassy.org.uk/eng* –Consulate General of the People's Republic of China: *Denison House | 71 Denison Road | Rusholme | Manchester M14 5RX | tel. 0161 22 48 672 | http://manchester.china-consulate.org/eng/*

US
– *Embassy of the People's Republic of China | 3505, International Place | N.W. Washington D.C. 20008 | USA | Consular dept.: tel. 0202 4 95 22 66 | http://www.china-embassy.org/eng/*

INFORMATION BEFORE YOU TRAVEL

CHINESE NATIONAL TOURIST OFFICE
– *71 Warwick Road | London SW5 9HB, UK | tel. 020 73 73 08 88 | www.cnto.org.uk*
– *350 Fifth Avenue, Suite 6413, Empire State Building | New York NY 10118, USA | tel. 0212 7 60 82 18 | www.cnto.org*

INFORMATION IN SHANGHAI

SHANGHAI CALL CENTER
The hotline 021 96 22 88 offers free and round the clock information in English about everything worth knowing in Shanghai e.g. addresses, transport, hospitals, cinemas, parks, stores, art centres, hotels, restaurants, bars and clubs. You can also book theatre tickets on this number. The staff are friendly and helpful and will, for example, translate English addresses into Chinese, so in the taxi you simply pass your mobile phone to the driver, which is a great help! *www.962288.com*

TOURIST INFORMATION & SERVICE CENTER

Tourist information is available in the Metro stations Railway Station South Exit (main railway station), People's Square and at Hongqiao Airport. Also: Jiujiaochang Lu 149 (134 C4) (∅ N7) | Nanjing Xilu 1612 (132 B2) (∅ H6) | Nanjing Donglu 561 (134 B2) (∅ M6). See also www.asiarooms.com/en/travel-guide/china/shanghai/shanghai-overview/shanghai-tourist-information-center.html

INTERNET ACCESS

You can surf the internet in the countless internet bars, in the Shanghai Library (Mon–Sat 9am–5pm | Huai-hai Lu 1555 | passport required) (132 A4) (∅ G8) and in the hotel business centres. Most hotels and lots of cafés offer free WI-FI access.

NEWSPAPERS & EVENTS

The English newspaper 'Shanghai Daily' (www.shanghaidaily.com) appears every day, the 'Shanghai Star' (www.shanghai-star.com.cn) weekly, both giving information about cultural events. Advice on events and addresses are also given in 'That's' which appears monthly (www.urbanatomy.com). Other magazines with events information are 'City Weekend' and 'Shanghai Talk'.

PHONE & MOBILE PHONE

You can phone abroad direct from your room in almost all hotels but, it has to be said, it's far from cheap. If you use a foreign mobile phone there are also high roaming charges. If you want to use your mobile phone quite often in China, you should buy yourself a SIM card (in all China Mobile stores and at the Kiosk, from 50 yuan); but check first that your mobile phone isn't blocked for other SIM cards. Phone cards are also available on the street. IC cards (Integrated Circuit, for 20, 50 and 100 yuan) are the cards for use in public call boxes. You can phone abroad quite reasonably with IP cards (Internet Phone card) from private phones, in some hotels and public call boxes, which are not card phones (simply dial the given number and follow the instructions).

For calls from abroad you dial for Shanghai +86 21, for Hangzhou +86 571 and for Suzhou +86 512, within China the dialling code (Shanghai 021, Hangzhou

CURRENCY CONVERTER

£	CNY	$	CNY
1	10	1	6.40
3	30	3	19
5	50	5	32
13	130	13	83
40	400	40	255
75	750	75	480
120	1,200	120	765
250	2,500	250	1,600
500	5,000	500	3,190

CNY	£	CNY	$
10	1	10	1.55
30	3	30	4.70
50	5	50	7.80
130	13	130	20
400	40	400	63
750	75	750	117
1,200	120	1,200	188
2,500	250	2,500	390
5,000	500	5,000	784

For current exchange rates see www.xe.com

0571, Suzhou 0512) and the number you want to call. For the UK dial +44, for USA +1, then the local dialling code without 0 and the number you want to call. Phone information in Shanghai: 114

POST

There are lots of post offices (where you can also get cardboard boxes for sending). But it's simpler to hand in your mail in your hotel. Airmail to Europe takes about a week.

PRICES & CURRENCY

The Chinese currency is the Renminbi (RMB). The unit of currency is the yuan (in rate of exchange lists also CNY), divided into ten Jiao (also Mao). The largest bank note is the one hundred. The rate of exchange of the yuan is linked to the US dollar. The gap between prices and income in Shanghai is huge. Food, taxis and clothes are in general very reasonably priced.

PUBLIC TRANSPORT

Excursion buses: Terminal at the *Shanghai Stadium | Tianyaoqiao Lu 666, Gate 5 | tel. 021 64 26 55 55 | M4 Shanghai Stadium (0) (𝄞 E12)*. Green tourist buses provide a daily service from 6.30am till the afternoon to the tourist attractions in and around Shanghai. Tickets can be bought direct from the driver as you board.

Rail: Travel by train is very reasonable. Tickets with seat reservations – *'hard seater'* (2nd class) or *'soft seater'* (1st class) – can be bought at the station, ordered in your hotel on payment of a surcharge or (two days before travel at the latest) booked in one of the many

WEATHER IN SHANGHAI

	Jan	Feb	March	April	May	June	July	Aug	Sept	Oct	Nov	Dec
Daytime temperatures in °C/°F												
	8/46	8/46	13/55	19/66	24/75	28/82	32/90	32/90	27/81	23/73	17/63	10/50
Nighttime temperatures in °C/°F												
	−1/30	0/32	4/40	9/48	14/57	19/66	23/73	23/73	19/66	13/55	7/45	2/36
Sunshine hours/day												
	4	4	4	5	5	5	7	8	5	6	5	4
Precipitation days/month												
	8	8	9	9	9	11	9	9	9	8	7	6

Train Ticket Booking Offices on payment of a fee of 5 yuan. At the railway station you can only buy a single ticket and you need your destination written down in Chinese characters.

Bus: Bus travel is very cheap (1–5 yuan) but not recommended without a reasonable knowledge of Chinese. Exception: the *bus line 911* which serves the route Hongqiao Lu–Huaihai Lu–Renmin Lu.

Metro: The metro network is very extensive and entrances can be recognised by a red 'M' on a white background. Tickets (3–8 yuan) are available from machines which also have an English menu. It is advisable to obtain an IC ticket *(Shanghai Public Transportation Card)* at one of the many *Service Points* in the metro stations, and you can top up the ticket at machines; there's a 20 yuan deposit which you get back when you hand in the ticket. You can then use the IC ticket to pay to travel on the metro, by taxi and bus without the need for cash. Stations are announced and signposted in English; additional information on maps and signs is abbreviated: North (N), South (S), East (E), West (W). The metro operates from 5am till approx. 11pm. There are lifts in the stations and usually also clean toilets. You'll find a metro map inside this book's back cover. When there's a station within walking distance of an address, this is indicated in the book.

SIGHTESEEING TOURS

Sightseeing tours: The state agency Jinjiang Tours offers half and full day tours with visits (250 or 400 yuan, booking one day in advance required). Departure is from the major hotels; if you show your taxi receipt, you'll get the fare reimbursed. On presentation of an official city plan (can be picked up free e.g. at the airport) you get a 50 yuan discount on the booking. *Daily 7am–7pm | Changle Lu 191/Corner Maoming Lu | tel. 021 64 45 95 25 | www.chinacityex.com* (133 D3) *(𝄞 J–K7)*

Harbour tours: Excursion boats are moored on the Bund level with Yan'an Donglu (135 D4) *(𝄞 O7)*. There are three-hour trips to the Yangtze Delta (mornings, afternoons), one- and two-hour tours, and the evening trips offer stunning views of the glittering city at night (35–100 yuan). *www.china-cruise.com/huangpu.htm* Guided tours of the city: At *www.shanghai-flaneur.com* you can book tours with specific themes (e.g. architecture or history, available in English of course).

TAXI

Taxis are normally only hard to get hold of in the morning and evening rush hours, or also if it rains. There are usually seat belts only in the front. Taxis have a registration number and a personal ID with photo on the dashboard and a taximeter. The basic price for the first 3 km/1.8 mi is 12 yuan, each additional kilometre costs 2.40 yuan, from 10km/6.2mi 3.60 yuan. At night (11pm–5am) taxis cost from 16 yuan. One of the largest companies is Dazhong *(tel. 021 9 68 22 | turquoise taxis)*. Shanghai Taxi Agency Hotline tel. *021 1 23 19*

TIME

China is eight hours ahead of the UK in winter and during BST seven hours ahead.

TIPPING

A tip is not expected in China. Exceptions: tour guides and page boys in luxury hotels. Taxi drivers will be pleased If you round up the fare.

USEFUL PHRASES CHINESE

PRONUNCIATION

Derived from simple pictographs, most Chinese characters have a meaning and phonetic component. But you don't have to understand them to speak the language. Pinyin (given below after the Chinese phrases) is a universal system of transliteration that makes things much easier. However, it is not always straightforward. Sounds to learn include the following consonants (initials) and vowels (finals), accompanied by their approximate English equivalents.

Initials
- *c* — like ts in 'its'
- *j* — like j as in 'jeer'
- *h* — like ch in Scottish 'loch'
- *q* — similar to ch as in 'cheer'
- *x* — similar to sh in 'she'
- *z* — like ds in 'kids'
- *zh* — like j in 'jug'

Finals
- *ao* — like ao as in 'how'
- *ai* — like y as in 'my'
- *ei* — like ay as in 'pay'
- *i* — after c, ch, r, s, sh, z, zh: just lengthens the initial sound, voiced; otherwise ee as in 'bee'
- *iao* — like ee-ow as in 'meow'
- *ou* — like ow as in 'show'

Please note: double and triple vowels are not separated, but spoken as one, so that, for example, 'shuang' or 'liao' are each just one syllable.

The four different tones in Mandarin Chinese are not always vital for understanding. But here they are if you'd like to try them out:

- ‾ 1st tone: high even pitch
- ´ 2nd tone: rising pitch, as if asking a question
- ˇ 3rd tone: falling pitch, then sharply rising, as if emphasising
- ` 4th tone: sharply falling, as if using an imperative

IN BRIEF	
Yes, correct/Yes, okay	对 [duì]/好 [hǎo]
No, wrong/No, not okay	不对 [bù duì]/不好 [bù hǎo]
Maybe	也许 [yě xǔ]
Thank you/You're welcome	谢谢 [xiè xie]/不谢 [bù xiè]
Please	请 [qǐng]

你会说汉语吗?

'Do you speak Chinese?' This guide will help you to say the basic words and phrases in Chinese.

Excuse me, please	对不起! [duì bu qǐ]
May I ...?	可以 ... 吗? [kě yǐ ... ma]
Pardon	请再说一遍 [qǐng zài shuō yī biàn]
I would like to .../ have you got ...?	我要 ... [wǒ yào]/ 有没有 ...? [yǒu méi yǒu]
How much is ...?	多少钱? [duō shao qián]
I like this/ I don't like this	我喜欢 [wǒ xǐ huan]/ 我不喜欢 [wǒ bù xǐ huan]
good/bad	好/不好 [hǎo/bù hǎo]
broken/doesn't work	坏了 [huài le]/不行 [bù xíng]
too much/much/little	太多/很多 [tài duō/hěn duō]/一点 [yī diǎn]
all/nothing	全部/都不要 [quán bù/dōu bù yào]
Help!/Attention!/ Caution!	救命!/注意! [jiù mìng/zhù yì]/ 小心! [xiǎo xīn]
ambulance	救护车 [jiù hù chē]
police/fire brigade	警察/消防队 [jǐng chá/xiāo fáng duì]
prohibited/forbidden	禁止 [jìn-zhǐ]
danger/dangerous	危险 [wēi xiǎn]
Can I take your picture?	可以照相吗? [kě yǐ zhào xiàng ma]

GREETINGS, FAREWELL

Good morning!/afternoon!	早上好!/你好! [zǎo shang hǎo /nǐ hǎo]
Good evening!/night!	晚上好!/晚安! [wǎn shàng hǎo /wǎn ān]
Hello! (greeting)	你好! [nǐ hǎo]
Hello! (telephone call)	喂! [wèi]
Goodbye/See you!	再见! [zài jiàn]
My name is ...	我叫 ... [wǒ jiào]
What's your name?	你贵姓? [nǐ guì xìng]
I am ... (American/English)	我是 ... (美国人/ 英国人) [wǒ shì ... (měi guórén/yīng guórén]

DATE & TIME

Monday/Tuesday	星期一/星期二 [xīng qī yī /xīng qī èr]
Wednesday/Thursday	星期三/星期四 [xīng qī sān/xīng qī sì]
Friday/Saturday	星期五/星期六 [xīng qī wǔ/ xīng qī liù]
Sunday/Working day	星期天/工作日 [xīng qī tiān /gōng zuòrì]
Holiday	假日 [jiàrì]

today/tomorrow/yesterday	今天/明天/昨天 [jīn tiān/míng tiān/zuó tiān]
hour/minute	小时/分钟 [xiǎo shí/fēn zhōng]
day/night/week	白天/晚上/星期 [bái tiān/wǎn shang/xīng qī]
month/year	月/年 [yuè/nián]
What time is it?	几点钟? [jǐ diǎn zhōng]
It's three o'clock	三点 [sān diǎn]
It's half past three	三点半 [sān diǎn bàn]

TRAVEL

open/	开放，营业中 [kāi fàng, yíng yè zhōng]/
closed	关闭 [guān bì]
entrance/vehicle entrance	入口 [rù kǒu]
exit/vehicle exit	出口 [chū kǒu]
departure/	开车 [kāi chē]/
departure (plane)/arrival	起飞/到达 [qǐ fēi/dàu dá]
toilets/ladies/gentlemen	洗手间/女/男 [xí shǒu jiān/nǚ/nán]
(no) drinking water	(非)饮用水 [(fēi) yǐn yòng shuǐ]
Where is ...?/Where are ...?	... 在那里? [zài nà li]
left/right	左/右 [zuǒ/yòu]
straight ahead/back	一直走/回去 [yīh zhí zǒu/huí qu]
close/far	远/近 [yuǎn/jìn]
bus/	公共汽车 [gōng gòng qì chē]/
stop	车站 [chē zhàn]
subway/	地铁 [dì tiě]/
taxi/cab	出租车 [chū zū chē]
street map/map	地图 [d ì tú]
train station/jetty/	火车站/码头[huǒ chē zhàn/mǎ tou]/
harbour	港口 [gǎng kǒu]
airport	机场 [jī chǎng]
schedule/ticket	时刻表/车票 [shí kè biǎo/chē piào]
single/return	单程/往返 [dān chéng/wǎng fǎn]
train (number)/	车次 [chē cì]/
track/platform	站台 [zhàn tái]
I would like to rent a bicycle	我想租自行车 [wǒ xiǎng zū zì xíng chē]

FOOD & DRINK

Could you please book a table for tonight for four?	我们今天晚上订四个人的位置 [wǒmen jīn tiān wǎn shang dìng sì gèrén de wèi zhi]
on the terrace	在外面 [zài wài miàn]

by the window	靠近窗户 [kào jìn chuāng hu]
The menu, please	请来菜单 [qǐng lái cài dān]
Could I please have ...?	請來 ... [qǐng lái]
bottle/carafe/ glass	一瓶/一听 [yī píng/yī tīng]/ 一杯 [yī bēh]
knife/fork	刀子/叉子 [dāo zi/chā zi]
spoon/chopstick	调羹/筷子 [tiáo gēng/kuài zi]
salt/pepper/sugar	盐/胡椒粉/糖 [yán/hú jiāo fěn/táng]
vinegar/soy sauce	醋/酱油 [cù/jàng yóu]
milk/lemon	牛奶/柠檬 [niú nǎi/níng méng]
cold/too salty/not cooked	冷了/太咸/不熟 [lěng le/tài xián/bù shú]
hot/cold/chilled (drink)	热的/冷的/冰的 [rè de/ lěng de/bīng de]
with/without ice	加冰块/不加冰块 [jiā bīng kuài/bù jiā bīng kuài]
sparkling/still	带气的/不带气的 [dāi qì de/bú dài qì de]
vegetarian/allergy	素食者/过敏 [sù shí zhě/guò mǐn]
May I have the bill, please?	买单 [mǎi dān]
receipt	发票 [fā piào]

SHOPPING

Where can I find...?	... 在那里? [zài nà li]
Do you put photos onto CD?	可以把照片烧录CD吗? [kě yǐ bǎ zhào piān shāo lù si-di ma]
pharmacy/chemist	药房 [yào fáng]
baker/grocer	面包店/菜市 [miàn bāo diàn/cài shì]
shopping centre/ department store	购物中心 [gòu wù zhōng xīn]/ 百货店 [bǎi huò diàn]
food shop	食品店 [shí pǐn diàn]
supermarket	超级市场 [chāo jí shì chǎng]
photographic items/ newspaper shop/kiosk	摄影器材店 [shè yǐng qì cái diàn]/ 書報亭 [shū bào tíng]
50 grammes/1 pound	一两/一斤 [yī liǎng/yī jīn]
100 grammes/1 kilo	一百克/一公斤 [yī bǎi kè/yī gūng jīn]
expensive/cheap/price	很贵/很便宜/价钱 [hěn guèh/hěn pián yi/djà-tjén]
more/less	多/少 [duō/schǎu]

ACCOMMODATION

I have booked a room	我预定了房间 [wǒ yù dìng le fang jiān]
Do you have any ... left?	还有房间吗? [hái yǒu fang jiān ma]
including breakfast?	包括早餐吗? [bāo kuò zǎo cān ma]

at the front/	朝马路 [cháo mǎl ù]/
seafront	有海景 [yǒu hǎi jǐng]
lakefront/	有湖景 [yǒu hú jǐng]/
river view	河景 [hé jǐng]
sit-down bath	浴室 [yù shì]
balcony/terrace	阳台 [jáng tái]
key/room card	钥匙/房卡 [yào sci/fang kǎ]
luggage/suitcase/bag	行李/箱子/包 [xíng lǐ/ziāng zi/bāo]

BANKS, MONEY & CREDIT CARDS

bank/ATM	银行/取款机 [yín háng/qǔ kuǎn jī]
pin code	密码 [mì mǎ]
I'd like to change ...	请给我兑换 … [qǐng gěi wǒ duì huàn …]
cash/Visa card/	现金/维士卡 [xiàn jīn/wéi shì kǎ]/
credit card/	信用卡 [xin yòng kǎ]
bill/coin	钞票/硬币 [chāo piào/yìng bì]
change	零钱 [líng qián]

HEALTH

doctor/dentist/	医生/牙医 [yī shēng/yá yī]/
paediatrician	儿科医生 [ér kē yī shēng]
hospital	医院 [yī yuàn]
fever/pain	发烧/痛 [fā shāo/tūng]
diarrhoea/nausea	拉肚子/杜子不舒服 [lā dù zi/dù zi bù shū fu]
sunburn	晒伤 [shài shāng]
inflamed/injured	发炎了/受伤 [fā yán le/shòu shāng]
plaster/bandage	膠布/敷布 [jiāo bù/fū bù]
ointment/cream	药膏/膏 [yào gāo/gāo]
pain reliever/tablet	止痛药/药片 [zhǐ tūng yào/yào piàn]
suppository	栓剂 [shuān jì]

POST, TELECOMMUNICATIONS & MEDIA

stamp/	邮票 [yóu piào]/
letter	信 [xìn]
postcard	明信片 [míng xìn piàn]
I would like an inter-national phone card	我要一张IC卡 [wǒ yào yī zhāng cí kǎ]
I'm looking for a prepaid card for my mobile	我要储值卡 [wǒ yào chǔ zhí kǎ]

Where can I find internet access?	在哪里可以上网? [zài nà li kě yǐ shàng wǎng]
What's the area code for ...?	... 区号多少? [qu hào duō shǎo]
dial/no connection/ engaged	拨/打不通 [bō/dǎ bù tōng]/ 占线 [zhàn xiàn]
socket/adapter/ charger	插箱/适配器 [chā xiāng/shì pèi qì]/ 变压器 [biàn yā qì]
computer/battery/ rechargeable battery	电脑/电池 [diàn nǎo]/ 电池 [diàn chí]
@-sign	小老鼠 [xiǎo lǎo shǔ]
internet address (URL)	网址 [wǎng zhǐ]
e-mail address	电子邮箱 [diàn zi yóu xiāng]
internet connection/ wifi	网线 [wǎng xiàn]/ 无线局域网 [wú xiàn jú yù wǎng]
e-mail/ print	打印电子信 [dǎ yìn diàn zi xìn]/ 打印文件 [dǎ yìn wén jiàn]

LEISURE, SPORTS & BEACH

beach/lido	海滩/海水浴场 [hǎi tān/hǎi shuǐ yù chǎng]
sunshade/lounger	阳伞/沙滩椅 [yang sǎn/shā tān yǐ]
low tide/high tide/current	高潮/低潮/巨流 [gāo cháo/dī cháo/jù liú]
cable car/chair lift	缆车/索道 [lǎn chē/suǒ dào]

NUMBERS

0	零 [líng]	15 十五 [shí wǔ]	
1	一 [yī]	16 十六 [shí liù]	
2	二 [èr]	17 十七 [shí qī]	
Two of them	两个 [liǎng gè]	18 十八 [shí bā]	
3	三 [sān]	19 十九 [shí jiǔ]	
4	四 [sì]	20 二十 [èr shí]	
5	五 [wǔ]	70 七十 [qī shí]	
6	六 [liù]	80 八十 [bā shí]	
7	七 [qī]	90 九十 [jiǔ shí]	
8	八 [bā]	100 一百 [yī bǎi]	
9	九 [jiǔ]	200 二百 [èr bǎi]	
10	十 [shí]	1000 一千 [yī qiān]	
11	十一 [shí-yī]	2000 两千 [liǎng qiān]	
12	十二 [shí èr]	10,000 一万 [yī wàn]	
13	十三 [shí sān]	½ 一半 [yī bàn]	
14	十四 [shí sì]	¼ 四分之一 [sì fēn zhī yī]	

NOTES

MARCO POLO TRAVEL GUIDES

ALGARVE
AMSTERDAM
ATHENS
AUSTRALIA
BANGKOK
BARCELONA
BERLIN
BRUSSELS
BUDAPEST
CALIFORNIA
CAMBODIA
CAPE TOWN
  WINE LANDS,
  GARDEN ROUTE
CHINA
COLOGNE
COPENHAGEN
CORFU
COSTA BLANCA
  VALENCIA
COSTA DEL SOL
  GRANADA
CRETE
CUBA

CYPRUS
  NORTH AND
  SOUTH
DUBAI
DUBLIN
DUBROVNIK &
  DALMATIAN COAST
EDINBURGH
EGYPT
FINLAND
FLORENCE
FLORIDA
FRENCH RIVIERA
  NICE, CANNES &
  MONACO
FUERTEVENTURA
GRAN CANARIA
HONG KONG
  MACAU
ICELAND
IRELAND
ISRAEL
ISTANBUL
JORDAN

KOS
KRAKOW
LAKE GARDA
LANZAROTE
LAS VEGAS
LISBON
LONDON
LOS ANGELES
MADEIRA
  PORTO SANTO
MADRID
MALLORCA
MALTA
  GOZO
MOROCCO
MUNICH
NEW YORK
NEW ZEALAND
NORWAY
OSLO
PARIS

PRAGUE
RHODES
ROME
SAN FRANCISCO
SARDINIA
SHANGHAI
SICILY
SOUTH AFRICA
STOCKHOLM
TENERIFE
THAILAND
TURKEY
TURKEY
  SOUTH COAST
TUSCANY
UNITED ARAB
  EMIRATES
VENICE
VIENNA
VIETNAM

- PACKED WITH INSIDER TIPS
- BEST WALKS AND TOURS
- FULL-COLOUR PULL-OUT MAP
  AND STREET ATLAS

STREET ATLAS

The green line [ ] indicates the Walking tours (p. 102–107)

All tours are also marked on the pull-out map

Photo: People's Square

Exploring Shanghai

The map on the back cover shows how the area has been sub-divided

Map labels

Row 1 (top):
町口足球场
Hongkou Stadium
Hongkou Football Stadium
Tomb of Lu Xun

D E

Pingxingguan
Huangshan
Xhaxing
Xibaoxing
Huxuan
Tongxin
Lu
Lu

Beilu Baochang Dongbaoxing Hengye
Yujingpu
Xijiangwan
Xijiangwan
Sichuan Beilu

Lu Xun Park
Memorial Hall of Lu Xun

1

2

Hengye Lu Zhonglu Huachang Handang Xijiangwan
Lu Baotong Tiantong'an
Huang qing
Sichuan Mid Sch
Former Residence of Lu Xun
Shanyin

Chinese Medicine Hospital
Xinlu Baochang Mid Sch
Hengbang Dongbaoxing Hailun
Duolun Duolun
Qingyuan Lu

HONGKOU

3

Tongge Lu
Gongxing Lufeng Hongyang
Normal School No. 3
Baotong Dongbaoxing Lu Yongming Lu
Dongbaoxing Rd
东宝兴路
People's Hospital Shanghai No. 1
Liyang
Tianshui

Linshan Lu
Baoyuan Chuangong Li Xinguang Xinxiang Lu Dongbaoxing
Changchun
Xitu Xinglaotao Beilu
Haitun Lu

ng Distance Bus Station
Qiujiang Baoshan Lu Xinguang Sichuan Xinglaoao Nanlu
Children's Park
Yujingpu

Baoshan Rd
宝山路
Gongqizhat Lu Zhilu Zhongzhou
Yedachang Commercial Bldg.
Hailun Lu
海伦路
Siping

ine)
Mid Sch Hengshui
Dongjiaxing
Liaoning
Liyang

u Donglu 天目东路
Dongxinmin Lu
Shanghai No.1 People's Hospital
Hsærbin
Mid Sch
Wujing Shanghai No.1 People's Hospital

Beilu Wujing Jiangxi
Lu
Yaliujiang Lu

4

5

Kangle Shanxi Beilu
Sichuan Rd N
Lu
Kunshan
Jiefang Theatre
Yuhang
Lu Buxing Liyang
Dongbao Do

Lu Haining
Penge Tanqu
Mid Sch
Lu Tangqu
Hongkou Branch

Henan Lu
Wuchang
Hanyang Mid Sch

Zhonglu Club
Sichuan Tiantong
Minhang Wuchang Emei
Changzhi

Tiantong Rd
Suzhou
Beilu
Shanghai Post Office
Suzhou
131
Broadway Mansions†
Union Church
135
Wusong
Daming 大名路
Astor House Hotel
Lu

Fujian Shanxi Beilu Zhonglu Hong Zhonglu Beilu
3
nghi

6

D | **E** | **F**

Jiangning Lu

Xilu

Beijing Lu

Chengdu Beilu

北

Fengxian Lu

Majestic Theatre

Isetan & Westgate Mall

German Consulate

Fengyang Lu

1

CITIC Square

Nanjing Beilu

Shimen 2-Lu

Wujiang

Fengyang Lu

Ping'an Art Cinema

Nanjing

Nanjing Rd W.
南京西路

Xilu

南北

Tomorrow Square

Shanghai Mandarin

Shanxi Beilu

Taixing Lu

Qinghai Lu

Jiangyin

2

Weihai

Beilu

Shanghai Second Polytechnic University

Maoming Beilu

Lu

Mid Sch

Shanghai TV Station

Chengdu Nanbei Gaojia Lu

Wusheng

Nanlu

Shimen 1-Lu

Weihai

Ruijin Theatre

Dagu

Square

Chongqing

Yan'an

d Children al, 1

Jinxian Lu

Lanxin Theatre

Julu

Square

Park

Lu

Danyin I-Lu X

3

Shanxi

Okura Garden Hotel

Jinjiang Tower

Ruijin 1-Lu

Changle

Mid Sch

Chengdu

Jinling

New World Mansion

Parkson Plaza

Jinjiang Hotel Cathay Theatre

Zhonglu

Nanchang

Xing'an

Yandang

i

Huangpi Rd Silu
黄陂南路

Taicang

Nanlu

Shanghai No.2 Department Store

Shanxi Rd S
陕西南路

St. Nikolaus Church

Scientific Seminar Hall

Xingye

XIN-TIAN

4

S

Gaolan Lu

Fuxing Park

Central Hospital of Luwan District

DI

Maoming Nanlu

Mid Sch

Xiangshan Lu

Former Residence of Dr. Sun Yat-Sen

Zizhong

Nanlu

Xintiandi

Zhonglu

Fuxing

Lu

卢湾

Ruijin Building

Shanghai Culture Centre

Former Residence of Zhou En-lai

Hefei

LUWAN

5

aoxing Lu

Ruijin Hospital

Medical University Shanghai No.2

Damshui

Yongnian

Kunju-Operahouse

2-Lu

Jiande

Zhonglu

Jianguo

Club

Chongqing

Stadium

Taikang Lu

Xilu

Jianguo

Lu

Yongnian

Huangpi

6

打浦桥
A PU QIAO

Ruijin

Jianguo

Zhonglu

Madang Rd
马当路

徐

家

Dapuqiao
打浦桥

Xujiahui

Xiexu

Chongqing Nanlu

Luban Lu
Nanbei Gaojia Lu

Mengzi

133

Madang

Huangpi

Liyuan

Mengzi

137

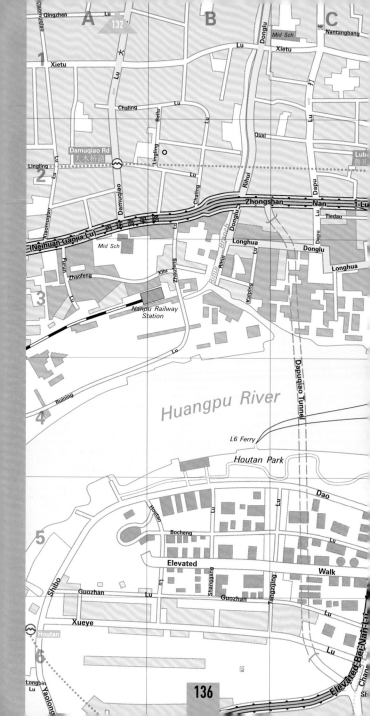

Xiaomuqiao
Qingzhen
Lu
Xietu
Donglu
Mid Sch
Xietu
Nantangbang

1

Xietu

Lu

Lu

Chaling

Beilu

Lu

Quxi

Damuqiao Rd
大木桥路

Lubz
鲁班

2

Lingling

Damuqiao

Lu

Chaling

Rihui

Rihui

Dapu

Zhongshan Nan 1-Lu

Tiedao

Dapu

(Neihuan Gaojia Lu) 西藏高架路

Lizi

Donglu

Longhua

Donglu

Longhua

Mid Sch

Xilu

Zhaofeng

Rihui Branch

Farun

Zhaofeng

Zhaofeng

Kaiping

Longhua

3

Nanpu Railway
Station

Lu

Ruining

Huangpu River

Dapuqiao Tunnel

4

L6 Ferry

Houtan Park

Dao

Houtan

Lu

Bocheng

Lu

5

Shangang

Elevated

Tangzijing

Walk

Sibo

Guozhan

Lu

Guozhan

Lu

Xueye

Houtan

Longbin
Lu

6

Yaolong

Elevated Bei Nan Lu

Chang

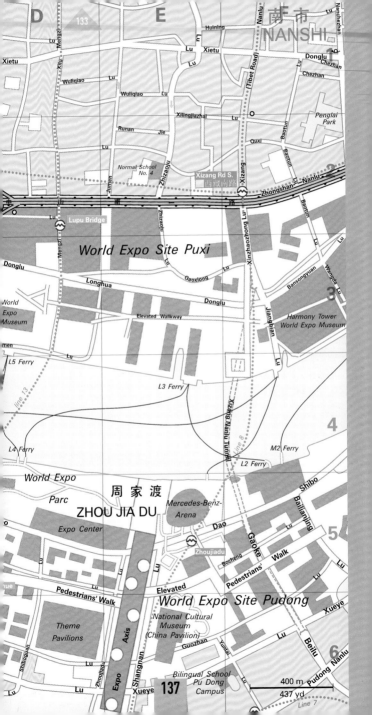

133

南市
NANSHI

Lu Nanchezhan
Huining
Lu Xietu Nanlu
Lu (Tibet Road) Donglu Chezhan
Xietu Lu Chezhan

Mengzi Xinyu Lu Xilingjiazhai Lu
Wuliqiao Lu
Wuliqiao Lu Baorun
Runan Jie Quxi Penglai
Lu Park
Normal School Baorun
No. 4 Xizang Rd S.
Zhizaolu 西藏南路 Xizang Zhongshan
Junmen Nanlu
Baorun Lu

Lu Lupu Bridge
Wengda Lu
World Expo Site Puxi
Donglu
Longhua Gaoxiong Lu Bansongyuan
Xinzhaozhong Lu
World Donglu
Expo Jiangbian Harmony Tower
Museum Elevated Walkway World Expo Museum

men
L5 Ferry
Lu

line 13 L3 Ferry Xizang Nanlu Tunnel
line 8

L4 Ferry M2 Ferry
L2 Ferry
World Expo Shibo
Parc 周家渡 Mercedes-Benz- Bailianjing
ZHOU JIA DU Arena
Expo Center Dao Gaoke Walk 5
Zhoujiadu Bocheng Pedestrians' Lu
Bilianjing
Pedestrians' Walk Elevated Xueye
World Expo Site Pudong
Lu National Cultural Lu
Museum Beilu
Theme (China Pavilion) Yundai
Pavilions Guozhan Pudong Nanlu
400 m
Bilingual School 437 yd
Shibaoguan Zhoujiadu Expo Axis Shangnan Xueye 137 Pu Dong
Campus Line 7

Lu
Lu

Xinmatou
Yongjiadu Hengjie
Donglu
Fuxing Donglu Tunnel
135
F
Dongqiao Building
Zhangyang Lu

aonanmen
南门
Fuxing
Laoxin

Jie

Line 9

Zhangyang

Binjiang Building

Fukang

Maojia Jie
Zixia
Welatamatou Hengjie
Xinmatou
Lu
Waima Jie
Jie
Lu
Cool Docks

Laoxin

Cxiontang

Fukang

Wangjiamatou
Doushi Jie
Belshilla
Long
Jie
Lu

Gaozi Lu

2

Xigouyu
Miezhu
Wancangqiao
Wanglamatou
Zhuhangmatou
Kemu
Wanyumatou
Gongyimatou
Jie
Jie

Pudian Lu

Divota
Nanpu
Jie
Lu
Xuejiabang Luxi
Dongjiadu Church
Nanlu
Huangjiadu

Zhangjiabang
Laobaidu

Xuejiabang
Jie
Xinjie
Xinmatou
Huangjian
Jie
Huangjiamatou

Nanzhangjiabang

3

Zhongshan
People's Hospital
Shanghai No. 2
Tangqiao
Line 2

Youchematou Jie
Waima

Tangqiao

Xinlu
Xilu
Tangqiao 塘桥
Nanlu
4

Nanpu Bridge
Inner Ring
Pudong

Xiaonanmatou
Pujian Lu
Pujian Lu

南码头
NAN MA TOU

Nanmatou
Jiaonan

Nanpu Square Park

PUDONG
5

Tangyan

Nanquan

Elevated

Line 6

Shanghai Children's Medical Center

Nanlu
400 m
437 yd

Shanghai Oriental TV

Dongfang Lu

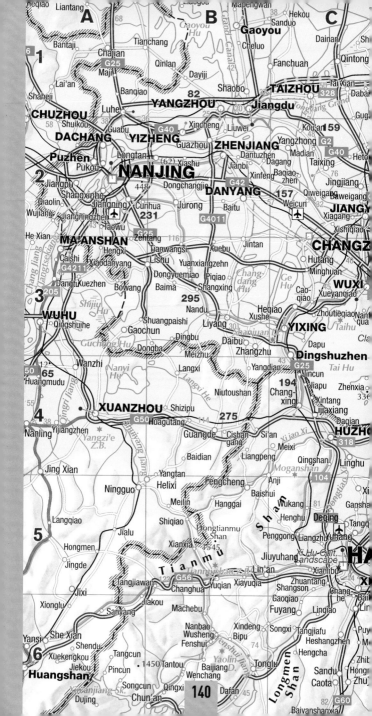

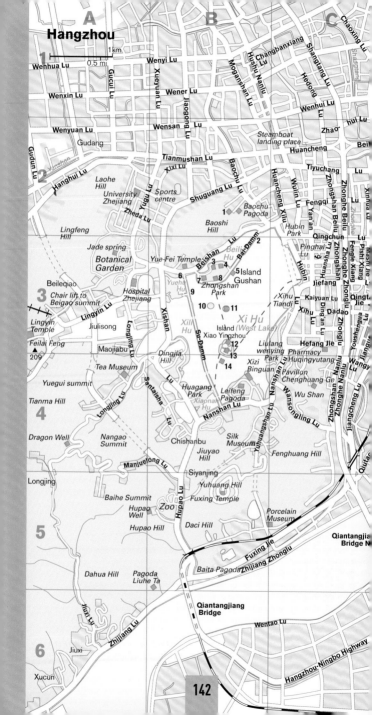

Hangzhou

1km
0.5 m

Wenhua Lu
Wenyi Lu
Wenxin Lu
Wenan Lu
Wener Lu
Xueyuan Lu
Jiaogong Lu
Changbanxiang
Shangtang Lu
Hedong
Moganshan Nanlu
Huhu Nanlu
Chaoxing Lu
Shadgtang
Wenhui Lu
Zhao
hui Lu
Bei
Wensan Lu
Gudang
Steamboat
landing place
Tianmushan Lu
Xixi Lu
Baochu Lu
Huancheng
Huancheng Xilu
Wulin Lu
Tiyuchang
Lu
Laohe Hill
Shuguang Lu
University Zhejiang
Sports centre
Baochu Pagoda
Zhonghe Beilu
Zheda Lu
1
Baoshi Hill
Fenggi
Zhongshan Beilu
Fengle Xiang
Xinhua Lu
Zhongde Zhonglu
Mashi Jie
Pishi Xiang
Lingfeng Hill
Jade spring
Beishan Lu
Beili Hu Ba Danm
2
Hubin Park
Qingchun Lu
Yanan Lu
Pinghai Lu
Zhongshan Zhonglu
Hssewn Lu
Qingt
Botanical Garden
Yue-Fei Temple
3 4 5 Island
Hubin
Jiefang
Dadao
Qing
Beileqiao
6
Gushan
7 8
Zhongshan Park
Xihu Tiandi
Kaiyuan Lu
Ding'an Lu
Dadao
Jie
Chair lift to Beigao summit
Hospital Zhejiang
Xishan
Yuehu Hu
9
10 11
Xi Hu (West Lake)
Xihu
Hefang Jie
Lingyin Temple
Jiulisong
Longjing Lu
Island Xiao Yingzhou
Liulang wenying Park
Pharmacy
Huqingyutang
Wangy
Feilai Feng
209
Maojiabu
Dingjia Hill
Si-Danm
12
13
Xizi Binguan
Pavillon Chenghuang Ge
Zhonghe Nanlu
Zhongshan Nanlu
Liangcheng Lu
Tea Museum
Santaisha
14
Leifeng Pagoda
Xiaonan
Wu Shan
Yuegui summit
Huagang Park
Wansongling Lu
Tianma Hill
Longjing Lu
Nanshan Lu
Nanshan Lu
Yuhuangshan Lu
Silk Museum
Fenghuang Hill
Dragon Well
Nangao Summit
Chishanbu
Jiuyao Hill
Manjuetong Lu
Siyanjing
Qiutao
Longjing
Baihe Summit
Hupao Well
Zoo
Hupeu Lu
Yuhuang Hill
Fuxing Temple
Porcelain Museum
Hupao Hill
Daci Hill
Qiantangjia Bridge N
Dahua Hill
Pagoda Liuhe Ta
Baita Pagoda
Zhijiang Zhonglu
Fuxing Jie
Jiuxi
Jiuxi Lu
Zhijiang Lu
Qiantangjiang Bridge
Wentao Lu
Xucun
Hangzhou-Ningbo Highway

Hangzhou

1 Sunrise Terrace
2 Duan Qiao Bridge
3 Sun Yat Sen Memorial Pagoda
4 Fanghe Pavilion (Crane Pavilion)
5 Pavilion 'Autumn Moon over the Calm Lake'
6 Lake stage 'Impression West Lake'
7 Qiu Jin's Grave
8 Provincial Museum
9 Dongpu Bridge
10 Ruangongdun Island
11 Pavilion 'In the Middle of the Lake'
12 Former 'Temple of the Soul's Retreat'
13 Greenhouse and bird house
14 Santan Yinyue

Suzhou

1 Zhuozheng Yuan Garden
    (Humble Administrator's Garden)
2 Bao'en Si Temple
3 Shizi Lin Garden (Lion Grove)
4 Liu Yuan Garden (Lingering Garden)
5 Ou Yuan Garden (Double Garden)
6 Yi Pu Garden (Garden of Cultivation)
7 Huanxiu Shanzhuang Garden
    (Mountain Villa with Embracing Beauty)
8 Xuanmiao Guan Temple
9 Opera and Theatre Museum
10 Yi Yuan Garden (Garden of Pleasure)
11 SuzhouPark
12 Tingfeng Yuan Garden
13 Canglang Ting Garden, Canglang Pavilion
14 Wangshi Yuan Garden
    (Garden of the Master of the Nets)

143

四車道公路 Vierspurige Straße		Road with four lanes Route à quatre voies
高架道路 Hochstraße		High level road Route surélevée
遠程公路 Durchgangsstraße		Thoroughfare Route de transit
主要公路 Hauptstraße		Main road Route principale
其它公路 Sonstige Straßen		Other roads Autres routes
信息 - 停車場 Information - Parkplatz	**i** **P**	Information - Parking place Information - Parking
單行公路 Einbahnstraße		One way road Rue à sens unique
步行區 Fußgängerzone		Pedestrian zone Zone piétonne
主要鐵路干綫, 火車站 Hauptbahn mit Bahnhof		Main railway with station Chemin de fer principal avec gare
其他鐵路干綫 Sonstige Bahn		Other railway Autre ligne
地下鐵道 U-Bahn		Underground Métro
渡輪航綫 - 停靠站 Fährlinie - Anlegestelle	⚓	Ferry line - Landing place Ligne de bac - Embarcadère
寺廟 - 寺廟, 風景區 Tempel - Sehenswerter Tempel	▲ ▲	Temple - Temple of interest Temple - Temple remarquable
教堂 - 教堂, 風景區 Kirche - Sehenswerte Kirche	✠ ✠	Church - Church of interest Église - Église remarquable
清真寺 - 猶太教堂 Moschee - Synagoge	☪ ✡	Mosque - Synagogue Mosquée - Synagogue
塔 - 青年旅社 Turm - Jugendherberge	♂ ▲	Tower - Youth hostel Tour - Auberge de jeunesse
警察局 - 郵局 Polizeistation - Postamt	● ☊	Police station - Post office Poste de police - Bureau de poste
醫院 - 紀念碑 Krankenhaus - Denkmal	✚ 요	Hospital - Monument Hôpital - Monument
建築, 公共建築 Bebaute Fläche, öffentliches Gebäude		Built-up area, public building Zone bâtie, bâtiment public
工業區 Industriegelände		Industrial area Zone industrielle
公園, 森林 Park, Wald		Park, forest Parc, bois
徒步觀光路線 Stadtspaziergänge		Walking tours Promenades en ville
MARCO POLO Highlight	★ 1	MARCO POLO Highlight

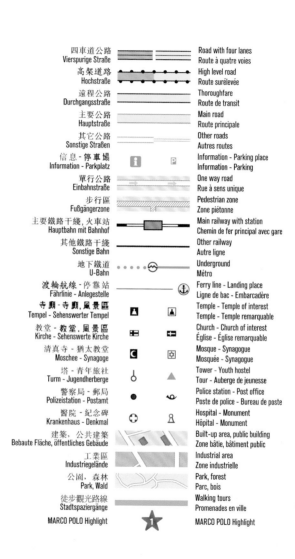

INDEX

The index contains all the sights, destinations and museums featured in this guide in Shanghai, Hangzhou and Suzhou. Page numbers in bold indicate a main entry.

WRITE TO US

e-mail: info@marcopologuides.co.uk

Did you have a great holiday?
Is there something on your mind?
Whatever it is, let us know!
Whether you want to praise, alert us
to errors or give us a personal tip –
MARCO POLO would be pleased to
hear from you.
We do everything we can to provide
the very latest information for your trip.

Nevertheless, despite all of our authors'
thorough research, errors can creep
in. MARCO POLO does not accept any
liability for this. Please contact us by
e-mail or post.

MARCO POLO Travel Publishing Ltd
Pinewood, Chineham Business Park
Crockford Lane, Chineham
Basingstoke, Hampshire RG24 8AL
United Kingdom

PICTURE CREDITS
Cover Photograph: Skyline (Getty Images/Vetta: Nikada)
Images: O. Bolch (104, 107); eno: Leon Ni (16 centre); R. Freyer (3 bottom, 24 r., 42/43, 49, 55, 61, 68, 70, 78, 82/83, 84, 90/91, 106); Fu Xin Gallery: Thomas Weuthen (16 top); Getty Images/Vetta: Nikada (1 top); Good-toChina (17 top); Huber: Picture Finders (108/109); © istockphoto.com: Olga Olejnikova (16 bottom); V. Janicke (110); Laif: China/PhotoPress (2 centre top, 9); Laif/Express-Rea: Dudoit (76); Laif/Le Figaro Magazine: Martin (114 top); mauritius: AGE (62 right, 64, 97, 98/99, 102/103, 114 bottom), Alamy (flap l., 3 top, 6, 8, 10/11, 12/13, 20/21, 23, 24 l., 30, 50, 52/53, 66/67, 110/111, 115), Bail (108), Buss (34), Hausberger (18/19), Mehlig (2 centre bottom, 26/27), Raga (7, 126/127), Vidler (111); mauritius images/imagebroker: Bail (15); Meadowbrook Equestrian and Rural Activity Center: Becky Tsukishima (17 bottom); p. Meyer-Zenk and H.- W. Schütte (1 bottom); Kai Ulrich Müller (44, 94/95); T. Stankiewicz (flap right, 2 top, 2 bottom, 3 centre, 4, 5, 25, 33, 37, 39, 41, 47, 56/57, 58, 62 l., 63, 72, 74/75, 81, 87, 88, 92, 94 top, 100, 109)

1st Edition 2013
Worldwide Distribution: Marco Polo Travel Publishing Ltd, Pinewood, Chineham Business Park, Crockford Lane, Basingstoke, Hampshire RG24 8AL, United Kingdom. Email: sales@marcopolouk.com
© MAIRDUMONT GmbH & Co. KG, Ostfildern
Chief editors: Michaela Lienemann (concept, managing editor), Marion Zorn (concept, text editor)
Author: Sabine Meyer-Zenk, Dr. Hans-Wilm Schütte; Editor: Corinna Walkenhorst
Programme supervision: Ann-Katrin Kutzner, Nikolai Michaelis, Silwen Randebrock
Picture editor: Gabriele Forst
What's hot: wunder media, Munich; Cartography street atlas: © MAIRDUMONT, Ostfildern;
Cartography pull-out map: © MAIRDUMONT, Ostfildern
Design: milchhof : atelier, Berlin; Front cover, pull-out map cover, page 1: factor product munich
Translated from German by Neil Williamson, Wilmslow; editor of the English edition: Tony Halliday, Oxford
Prepress: BW-Medien GmbH, Leonberg
Phrase book in cooperation with Ernst Klett Sprachen GmbH, Stuttgart, Editorial by Pons Wörterbücher

DOS & DON'TS ✋

A few things and situations you should avoid in Shanghai

TRAVELLING ON BANK HOLIDAYS

The whole of China closes down for a holiday for the Spring Festival, Labour Day and National Day. Packed trains, fully booked hotels and crowded sights can turn a nice day out into a nightmare.

UNDERESTIMATING THE TRAFFIC

Every month some 7,500 new vehicles are licensed in Shanghai, which means only one thing: the traffic jams are going from bad to worse. So always allow plenty of time for your journey.

GETTING RIPPED OFF

Beware of unsolicited city guides! A favourite trick is persuading visitors to allow themselves to be taken to a teahouse or restaurant where they're then presented with an outrageous bill. If you go to a karaoke bar or massage parlour, find out in advance about the nature and costs of the services provided because, although prostitution is illegal, it's practised both here and in hair salons. Rotating lights at the entrance are often an indication that sexual services are also offered. The annoying touts trying to sell fake goods in backrooms are also after only one thing – to rip you off.

BELIEVING EVERYTHING TRADERS TELL YOU

If you buy an item, then do so because you like it but not because it's apparently old or genuine or is supposed to be valuable for some other reason. Hardly any of the designer handbags you're offered are made of leather, and the luxury watches will soon stop working.

SETTING OFF WITHOUT A WRITTEN ADDRESS

You should always have the address you're heading for written down in Chinese characters. If it's not listed in this book, then get someone in your hotel to write it down for you! Collect bilingual visiting cards everywhere you go and from everyone you meet. It's unusual for taxi drivers to speak English and they can't read our alphabet. Also, be aware that English (hotel) names are usually not a translation of the Chinese name.

BUYING BOOTLEG GOODS

If you do so, you can have real difficulties with the Chinese customs. If you then have to pay import duty on return to the UK or USA on your supposedly genuine Gucci handbag, it wasn't worth buying in the first place.

GETTING CAUGHT OUT BY THE SHOE SHINE BOYS

Especially in the area round People's Square, there's a gang working which attracts customers with a price of 'only ten!' When your shoes are then gleaming, it's not ten Yuan that they want but ten dollars. So agree in advance a fixed price because there are also honest shoe shine boys. Should you think someone is trying to pull a fast one, then simply threaten to call the police and you'll soon be rid of him.